A Manual for the Early Years SENCO

Collette Drifte

P·C·P

Paul Chapman
Publishing

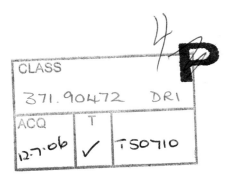
© Collette Drifte 2005

First published 2005

Paul Chapman Publishing
A SAGE Publications Company
1 Oliver's Yard
55 City Road
London EC1Y 1SP

SAGE Publications Inc
2455 Teller Road
Thousand Oaks, California 91320

SAGE Publications India Pvt Ltd
B-42, Panchsheel Enclave
Post Box 4109
New Delhi 110 017

Library of Congress Control Number: 2005926680

A catalogue record for this book is available from the British Library

ISBN 1-4129-1025-0
ISBN 1-4129-1026-9 (pbk)

Typeset by Pantek Arts Ltd, Maidstone, Kent
Printed in Great Britain by Cromwell Press Ltd, Trowbridge, Wiltshire

Contents

Acknowledgements   vii

Biographical details   ix

Introduction   xi

1 The SENCO year – a bit of forward planning goes a long way   1

2 Policy and practice – the unbroken circle   11

3 Supporting colleagues – giving help where it's needed   23

4 Supporting the children – making sure their entitlements are met   59

5 Keeping track – ensuring effective record keeping   89

6 A parent thing – maintaining a collaborative partnership   109

7 Coming together – the teamwork approach   128

Glossary of some educational acronyms   141

Further reading   143

Index   145

Acknowledgements

My thanks always go firstly to the children and practitioners who have taught me so much over the years – they're all very special people.

Thanks, too, go to my editor and friend, Jude Bowen, for her quiet and efficient professionalism and constant support – her faith in me has been an important part of the writing of this book.

And last but not least, thanks to Reinhard, especially for taking over on the days when I had to write and do nothing else!

Biographical details

Collette Drifte is a freelance author and trainer, with 22 years' experience in mainstream and special education. A former deputy head teacher and now living in Northumberland, she has written numerous articles and books in the fields of early years special needs and early years literacy. She speaks regularly at national conferences and exhibitions and leads courses, workshops and seminars across the country.

For Simon and Angela Frampton, with my love

Introduction

This book was written in response to a request that I've heard many times from newly appointed Special Educational Needs Coordinators (SENCOs): *I've never done this before – is there a manual or guidebook in Easyspeak that I can get hold of?*

SENCOs are proliferating; they're everywhere now, having been appointed to all early years settings and provision. Sadly, many of them feel they've drawn the short straw, have been pushed in at the deep end and are totally overwhelmed by the enormity of their responsibilities. They really shouldn't be feeling that way, but if that's how you feel too, then this book is for you! It aims to help and support you, to outline in reader-friendly language exactly what you're supposed to do as your setting's SENCO, and, above all, to enable you to realise you don't have to struggle on your own.

This book shows you how to help and support your colleagues, but also how to access the help and support you may feel you need yourself. It explores your roles and responsibilities as outlined in the *Special Educational Needs (SEN) Code of Practice*, and how these are relevant to the early years sector. Each chapter addresses in detail one of those roles, and the issues behind putting that particular role into practice.

SENCOs work within a huge variety of early years provision, everything from a 'standard' nursery school or class with several practitioners, to a single childminder with a few little ones in their care, from a small village playgroup to a large day nursery offering care from birth to four or five years. Clearly it's impossible to address every type of provision in detail, and therefore some of the advice in this book may need to be adapted to suit your individual needs. However, the book's overall content is there as a framework for you to tweak, adopt, adapt or use as a kick-off (i.e. for you to cherry-pick), to help you formulate practices that will not only make you an efficient SENCO, but, more importantly, will give you confidence in your role, and also help you feel comfortable and happy in it.

I have written the book on the assumption that you are a SENCO completely new to the job and that you're looking for ideas in each area of responsibility in your role. If, however, you're becoming an old(er) hand at the game, you could skip the bits you're conversant with and go to the sections you want to focus on, since each chapter is freestanding, and you won't have to wade through pages of text to get to the core of your question. The format of each chapter is the same: an outline of the key points addressed, a short introduction, the main body of the chapter and the issues it's exploring, followed by a summary. There are also photocopiable resources where relevant.

Now a few words about terminology. Throughout the book I refer to 'children with special educational needs' or 'children with additional needs', because they are just that: children first and foremost, who happen to have a difficulty, problem or disability. I still hear reference to, for example, 'an autistic child' or 'a Down's child', comments which show how deeply entrenched the practice still is of identifying a child by their disability. That disability is (or should be) secondary to the child's right and entitlement to be automatically perceived principally as a child, a human being who happens to have differing needs from the majority of their peers. I refer to 'special educational needs' with reservation, and use the term mainly because it's the common currency within the field, and it's the terminology of the SEN and disability legislation. Some groups representing the world of the disabled (their preferred term) are lobbying to have the phraseology within the legislation altered, but until that happens, we may have to continue using the SEN terminology on many occasions. That doesn't mean, however, that we can't use phrases such as 'differing needs' or 'additional needs' in our everyday dealings. Use the terminology that you're comfortable with, but make sure it's not offensive or derogatory.

Let's consider next what a SENCO needs, to do the job effectively. Apart from you being a sort of early years Houdini, your diplomatic, social, organisational, humanitarian and specialist skills need to be developed, alert and active at any given moment! The Pre-school Learning Alliance (2002) sums up very well what the minimum specifications of a SENCO should be:

Knowledge and understanding

- Diploma in Pre-school Practice or equivalent level 3 qualification
- Knowledge and understanding of the DfES SEN Code of Practice
- Knowledge of relevant legislation
- Sound understanding of child development, and of children's needs
- Understanding and implementation of equal opportunities.

Experience

- Experience of implementing the requirements of the SEN Code of Practice
- 3 years' experience of working in a pre-school setting
- Experience of contributing to the development of Individual Education Plans
- Experience of participating in reviews
- Experience of working with very young children with SEN and their families
- Experience of working in a multi-disciplinary team.

Skills

- Sound observation and record-keeping skills

- Ability to plan and implement Individual Education Plans

- Ability to plan and participate in reviews

- Ability to write clear reports

- Ability to work with a range of professionals

- Ability to work with parents and encourage their involvement in their child's learning

- Ability to work in a team and to lead a team of adults.

Some specialist pre-schools may demand additional knowledge and expertise in their area of specialist provision. This should also be indicated in the person specification. [1]

Now before you wail in despair and say, *I'm not all those, I can't be all those and I haven't done all those,* have a think about your experience and expertise as a mainstream early years practitioner. You'll have worked closely with parents, colleagues and other professionals. You'll have attended and/or organised meetings, parents' evenings or case conferences. You'll have kept up to date with your records, portfolios, files and profiles. You'll have planned activities, lessons or sessions, adapting and differentiating them to ensure all the children were included. You'll have written reports, recommendations and résumés. By definition, you're an early years practitioner because you have your qualification(s) and knowledge and experience of child development. So, at the end of the day, these specifications of a SENCO aren't a million miles removed from your present situation. If there's an area or two in which you'd like to expand your knowledge and/or experience, ask for the means to do it – if you need it to fulfil your SENCO role effectively, then you should receive it!

One of the most important things to remember is that **you do not have to do everything yourself**. It isn't your job to implement the Individual Education Plans (IEPs) (except where they're for one of 'your' children) or to train your colleagues (unless you have that specific brief because of an extra qualification, for example) or to draw up the SEN policy. You're there as a **coordinator** and as such, you can enable your colleagues to take on board and carry out *their* responsibilities. So don't try to be all things to all people, because you'll end up being of no help to anybody, particularly the children. I hope that this book will enable you to find the ways there are of getting help and support, not only for your colleagues but also for yourself – especially for yourself. If only one or two SENCOs finish this book feeling more confident and with a better belief in themselves, then I'll be a happy author!

References

1 *The Role of the Special Educational Needs Co-ordinator in Pre-school Settings* (The Pre-school Learning Alliance, 2002).

Chapter 1

The SENCO year – a bit of forward planning goes a long way

The **key points** covered in this chapter are:

- Practical strategies for making life as a SENCO both organised and easier.

- Planning the year ahead.

- Statutory assessment – following the timetable.

INTRODUCTION

By taking time to plan an overview of the year ahead, you'll be giving yourself an easy reference, set-out agenda that will make your life as a SENCO much easier, especially once you're into the busy roll of activities that are woven into the life of an early years setting.

The *Special Educational Needs (SEN) Code of Practice* has an inbuilt timetable for implementing Individual Education Plans (IEPs), holding reviews (whether of Differentiated Learning Plans [DLPs], IEPs or of Statements of Special Educational Needs) and carrying out statutory assessments. For example, it states that everybody involved in a review must have a fortnight's notice of the review date; they must also have sufficient time to prepare their reports or comments, and to submit or circulate these beforehand.

Keeping up to date with these timed commitments can be difficult and stressful, particularly if your setting has several children whose programmes are operating at different times across the year. Here we'll explore how to plan well ahead of time, enabling you to have a 'glance-at' system that keeps you up to speed.

PRACTICAL STRATEGIES FOR MAKING LIFE AS A SENCO ORGANISED AND EASIER

Assuming you're starting from scratch, it's a good idea first to have a look at your position as SENCO, in the context of your setting. As we discussed in the Introduction, no single book can address the needs of every early years setting, since there's such a variety of provision on offer these days. However, have a look at the following questions – cherry-pick those that are relevant and appropriate to your situation – and use your answers to focus your thoughts on what you already have and what you might need.

- Are you confident and comfortable in your role as SENCO?

- If not, can you say why?

- Have you received sufficient training?

- Have you received effective training?

- If not, can you access training of the type and standard you require?

- Does your daily/weekly routine enable you to have sufficient dedicated SENCO-time? If not, can you address this?

- Does your setting acknowledge your position as SENCO, e.g. by awarding you recognised status, influence, time, resources, finances, support, etc.?

- Do your setting's resources, equipment, facilities and structure enable you to support children with additional needs effectively?

- Do they enable you to practise inclusion fully and effectively?

- If not, can you address the reasons why not?

- Are you confident in your abilities to support your colleagues and meet their needs in relation to including children with SEN?

- If not, why not? And what can be done about it?

- Have your colleagues received sufficient and effective training?

- If not, can they access it, or can you access it for them?

- Do you feel supported and valued in your setting by (a) your management team, (b) your colleagues, (c) your Local Education Authority (LEA) or other authority's provision and facilities?

- Do you feel ineffective and/or unable to carry out your role as SENCO? If so, make a list of the reasons why and decide what can be addressed immediately, what's short-term, medium-term and long-term.

- Do you have the opportunity to meet with other SENCOs regularly for mutual support, exchange of ideas, sharing of best practice, etc.? If not, can you do something about it?

Keep your answers on file, and revisit them after nine months or so (date your original answers). If you find that you're making progress with your situation, that's fine. If, however, you find that your answers seem to be the same, or haven't changed much, it might be a good idea to review your situation with your management colleagues, highlighting the areas you feel need to be developed. Use the questionnaire above to support your case.

Nuts and bolts (well – maybe a filing cabinet and photocopier)

Let's have a look now at the down-to-earth stuff. If you're a newly appointed SENCO and wondering where to start, don't despair – just start at the beginning, decide what you need and ask for it!

Here's a starter list:

- *An efficient, confidential and lockable filing system.* Depending on your needs, this could be a filing cabinet with two or three drawers, a small cupboard or even a dedicated drawer within the main, larger filing system. But stake a claim to some SENCO and/or SEN-only space. If you're really lucky, your setting may even give you an area of your own … (dare I say *An office?*).

- *Folders for the children's records.* Here you should decide as a staff whether to incorporate a section within the child's main folder that's designated for their SEN documentation, or whether you want a separate SEN folder. As a team, decide how you want to file the folders, e.g. by level of the *SEN Code of Practice*, by age group, by setting group, by key worker, in alphabetical order, etc. Don't forget to decide on the type of folder, e.g. ring binders, manila wallets, plastic folders, etc. Your budget will probably help in this decision!

- *Coloured stickers.* You can use these on the outside of each child's folder, to show at a glance what stage of the *SEN Code of Practice* the child has reached, e.g. a blue sticker for 'Expression of Concern/Differentiated Learning', a green sticker for 'Early Years Action', a yellow sticker for 'Early Years Action Plus' and a red sticker for 'Statutory Assessment'. As the child moves through the different levels, simply put a sticker of the next colour onto the front of the folder.

- *Ring binders and clear plastic insert-wallets.* Use these to file summary sheets, forms, registers, etc. that are currently in use – in other words, the everyday working documents containing information you may want to check frequently and quickly. You might decide as a setting that everybody should have duplicate files with copies of the same information. Make sure all colleagues keep all files and records in secure and confidential places.

- *Wallets for blank pro forma, record sheets, letters, etc.* Keep them well stocked up – there's nothing more irritating than going for a form or review sheet only to find the wallet empty. Have a rule that says whoever takes out the last form should make several more photocopies and leave them in the wallet for future users.

● *A wall calendar with every day on it.* Depending on your setting, you'll need one that shows either the whole year (January to December) or the academic year (September to August). Keep it displayed so that all staff can see at a glance what's happening in relation to the 'additional needs events', but display it in a confidential place and position.

The paper chase

By definition, you'll have a lot of paperwork to store. Much of it will be record forms – blank ones, completed ones, and 'sleeping' ones waiting to be finally discarded – but which ones? Here's a list:

● Observation forms

● Assessment sheets/baselines/checklists etc.

● Expression of Concern forms

● Differentiated Learning Plan (DLP) forms

● Play Plan forms

● Home/setting communication forms or system

● Activity report sheets

● Individual Education Plan (IEP) forms

● Review forms

● Summary sheets

● Referral forms (a) to outside agents, (b) for Statutory Assessment

● Educational advice forms (usually supplied by the LEA)

● Statements of Special Educational Needs

● Letters.

You'll also need to keep in the file your setting's SEN documents and information, and all the documentation from the LEA, outside agents, voluntary bodies, etc. that your colleagues may need. *What documentation?* you might ask. Here's a list:

● Your SEN policy (long and short versions, where appropriate)

● The LEA's SEN policy and all relevant circulars, directives and documentation issued locally

● Parent Partnership documents

● Sure Start (or Early Years Development and Childcare Partnership [EYDC]) documents relating to additional needs

● Contact details of parent support groups, translators, alternative communication agents, etc.

- The *SEN Code of Practice* and the *SEN Toolkit*, plus other relevant and current government circulars regarding additional needs

- Contact details, prospectuses, policies, etc. of outside agents and/or other departments, e.g. social services, health, etc.

- In-service training (INSET) materials and other relevant photocopiables, documentation, etc. (where relevant).

If you keep the logistical aspects of the job organised and easy to use, life as a SENCO will be less fraught. It *is* a demanding job, and you don't need the added stresses of trying to find records, contact details, local procedures, etc. which are lost in a heap of damp documents piled up on the work surface in the Water Play area!

Planning the year ahead

It will depend on your setting what and how you need to plan. For example, if you're a SENCO in a large primary school, you'll have more manpower, time and resources than if you're SENCO in a playgroup or for a group of childminders. You'll need to assess what you have and how you can exploit it, in order to do the job effectively. There's no doubt that the role of SENCO involves plenty of paperwork, so getting this under control must be one of your priorities. If you and your computer have a close relationship, use a good spreadsheet program to plan the year ahead. Setting up the calendar at the beginning may involve a bit of investment of your time, but once the job's done, all you'll need to do in future years is tweak the fine details.

Divide the jobs into less frequent ones (the annual or biannual happenings) and frequent ones (the ongoing daily, weekly or monthly stints, or those that happen every three months/each term) and decide which are happening when. Decide too which dates are non-negotiable and log these onto the calendar before you do anything else. Let's have a look at this in more detail.

Less frequent jobs

First of all, identify the whole-setting jobs and commitments that take place across the year. Here's a list, some of which may not apply to you, depending on your setting:

- Whole-setting assessment sessions, e.g. medical and/or dental checks, baseline/checklist assessments for mass admissions, etc.

- INSET sessions (your own and/or your colleagues') and the dates these are scheduled

- Annual reviews of Statements of Special Educational Needs, and biannual reviews where relevant

- Annual and/or three-monthly/termly commitments involving the children, e.g. trips, outings, visits, the photographer, pantomimes and other social events, etc.

● Times where you can expect large numbers of children to be absent, e.g. high season holiday periods, etc.

Log onto your calendar any dates that you know are definite, even if those booked for much later in the year are rescheduled or cancelled. This will help you to avoid double booking. By keeping the year planner near the telephone, you can see at a glance whether a suggested date made by your caller is convenient.

● Frequent jobs

Next, identify the events that happen every three months (or every term), every month or every week. Among these might be:

● your own regular meetings, e.g. staff meeting every Thursday afternoon, meeting on the third Wednesday of the month with other SENCOs, Parent/Staff Group meetings every fourth Monday afternoon, etc.;

● regular and/or arranged visits by outside agents, e.g. the health visitor calls every other Monday, the educational psychologist calls on the first Tuesday after each half-term holiday, etc.;

● reviews of DLPs, Play Plans, IEPs, etc., whether these are every six weeks or every three months, as appropriate;

● the setting's SEN policy review meetings;

● meetings with governors (if appropriate to you);

● parents' open days or evenings (if appropriate).

Again, log these onto the year planner and once they're in place, you can play with the free dates for other meetings or reviews, etc. that crop up as the year rolls along. It's a good idea to get into the habit first thing every Monday of checking the week's bookings, commitments and jobs on the 'to do' list.

Also check:

● the review schedule for the fourth week from where you are, and log in all the 'to dos' for each review, on the relevant date. For a more detailed discussion of these 'to dos', see the section *IEP reviews* in Chapter 4, page 66;

● this week's IEP listings to see who's been on what level and for how long;

● whether there are any meetings to arrange regarding these IEPs;

● whether any outside agents are due to make support visits.

By now, your year planner will be starting to fill up a bit, and you'll begin to see why it's such a good idea to have an overview of what's happening on your additional needs agenda.

Figure 1.1 shows an example of a completed month from a Year Planner Form.

Figure 1.1 An example of a completed month from a Year Planner Form

MON	TUES	WED	THURS	FRI	SAT	SUN
	1	2 David Jones's docs all in yet?	3 3.30: Policy review – whole staff	4	5	
6 Suzie Scott's docs all in yet? 3.30: SENCO meeting	7	8 Biscuits etc. for David's review?	9 Send invites & docs for Suzie Scott's review (23rd)	10 10.00: David Jones's IEP review	11	12
13 Ask for docs for Sam Brown's review (due 10.04.05)	14	15 Vikki B's IEP 3 wks old – check progress	16	17 10.00: Ed. Psych. re: John F. (Mum coming)	18	19
20	21	22 Biscuits etc. for Suzie's review?	23 10.00: Suzie Scott's IEP review	24	25	26
27 9.00 – 3.30. Staff SEN training day	28	29 Mrs Smith's group on farm visit	30 pm: Easter Bonnet contest	31 Ask for docs for Gita Rani's review (due 28.05.05)		

© Collette Drifte, *A Manual for the Early Years SENCO*, Paul Chapman Publishing, 2005

Once you've filled in the immoveable feasts on your year planner, you'll then need to update it on at least a weekly basis. If you can, get into the habit of checking each evening whether you marked up something that was arranged during the day. It's so easy in the hubbub of a busy early years setting to come off the phone and be so distracted by one of the children marmelising another, that you forget to make a note in the diary of an arranged visit or review meeting, or whatever. Taking a few minutes in the quiet at the end of the day will keep you up to speed, and may even save you some embarrassment later when everybody turns up for a review meeting that you'd completely forgotten about!

STATUTORY ASSESSMENT – FOLLOWING THE TIMETABLE

Because the *SEN Code of Practice* gives a specific timetable for Statutory Assessments and the issuing of Statements of Special Educational Needs, you might find it a good idea to have a separate calendar or diary dedicated to this level of the process. The days on a routine year planner can look quite busy and crowded over time and you may miss an important date in the schedule of a Statutory Assessment. Having a dedicated planner will avoid this. Again, a computer spreadsheet or even a simple wall hanging calendar will do nicely.

Once you have a child going down the Statutory Assessment route, mark on the calendar the dates of what should be happening when. You can work these out by looking at the flow chart on page 120 of the *SEN Code of Practice* and calculating the appropriate dates from the date your child's referral was received by the LEA. You can check this by ringing them to confirm receipt and on what date. So, for example, if your child's referral was received by the LEA on 3rd March, the obligatory timetable is this:

Figure 1.2

	3 March	LEA receives referral
by	**14 April**	LEA must decide whether to assess (i.e. within 6 weeks)
by	**23 June**	LEA asks for and receives advice, and must decide whether to make a Statement of Special Educational Needs (i.e. over the next 10 weeks, which is 16 weeks from receipt of referral)
by	**7 July**	LEA must issue either draft Statement or reasons for not making a Statement (i.e. within the next 2 weeks, which is 18 weeks from receipt of referral)
by	**1 September**	LEA must issue final Statement (i.e. within the next 8 weeks, which is 26 weeks from receipt of referral)

The dates on your wall calendar could therefore look something like this:

Figure 1.3

3 March	LEA received Jade Kirby's referral (confirmed on phone 8 March – spoke to Kelly Blythe, SEN Dept.)
14 April	Has LEA decided whether to assess Jade Kirby? If not, chase.
28 April	Has LEA requested educational advice re: Jade Kirby yet? If not, chase.
23 June	Has LEA received advice re: Jade Kirby? Has it decided whether to make Statement? If not yet notified, chase.
7 July	Has LEA issued draft Statement or reasons for not making a Statement for Jade Kirby? If not, chase.
1 September	Has LEA issued Jade Kirby's final Statement? If not, chase.

Once the child's Statement of Special Educational Needs has been issued, there'll be a strict timetable of reviews. Usually the LEA convenes these reviews so, while as SENCO you organise in-house review meetings, you're unlikely to be expected to do the Annual or Biannual reviews. However, you'll still need to collate the paperwork, educational advice and feedback from all the involved agents within the setting.

Above all, you must continue to make sure the child's parents are being kept informed, advised of their rights and consulted for their opinion. They may need extra support during this time, so it's important you check whether they're comfortable with the process and fully understand what's happening. And, of course, it goes without saying that the child continues to receive support and help too.

The legislation requires an Annual Review, to be held on the anniversary of the issue of the Statement. For very young children, an interim review is also held (i.e. every six months) although on a less formal level. Because the needs and development of children in the early years stage can change rapidly and fundamentally, their progress must be monitored very closely and reviewed more often than older children's.

From the content of this chapter, you can see it's not rocket science to get an organised and smoothly run schedule. As with all things, time and effort invested in the beginning will pay dividends in the end. Once you have a system in place that you're comfortable with, and that you find easy to run, much of the paper chasing that the SENCO's role demands will be manageable. Don't become frustrated if you haven't got it all in place within 24 hours. Take time to let your system 'bed down', so you can see how and where it works for you, and where it's causing you a headache; look at it again and see how you can change it to suit your needs.

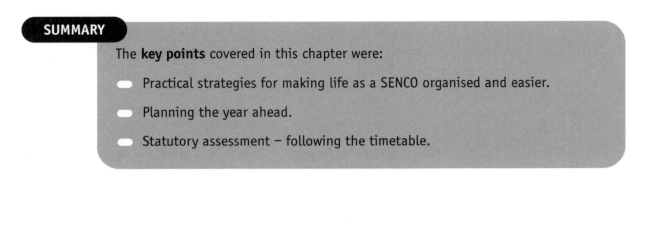

SUMMARY

The **key points** covered in this chapter were:

- Practical strategies for making life as a SENCO organised and easier.
- Planning the year ahead.
- Statutory assessment – following the timetable.

Chapter 2

Policy and practice – the unbroken circle

The **key points** covered in this chapter are:

- The policy/practice issue – which comes first?
- The difference between inclusion and integration.
- Policies as working documents, constantly under review.
- The role of the SENCO in policy development and implementation.
- What needs to go into an inclusive special educational needs (SEN) policy?
- Planning and implementing an inclusive SEN policy – some practical ideas.

INTRODUCTION

Here we'll be exploring an overview of SEN policy issues. If you're new to the concept, this chapter should answer your queries, worries and questions about 'how it's done'. It isn't rocket science and by the end of the chapter I hope you'll feel confident in helping your setting to write a good, inclusive policy.

THE POLICY/PRACTICE ISSUE – WHICH COMES FIRST?

The *SEN Code of Practice* states that all early years settings receiving government funding must write and put into practice an SEN policy. But aside from the legal requirement, writing such a policy is an excellent way for you to review your practices and philosophy, and to focus on inclusion. For this reason, private and non-maintained settings also need to write and implement their own SEN policies.

If you're due to be inspected by *Ofsted* you may feel pressurised into writing the policy so it's ready to show. It's important not to give in to this pressure, since you could end up with a poorly planned policy that does everything but ensure the children's entitlements. If you're in the early stages of the process, note in your action plan document your intention to formulate your SEN policy in the short to medium term, or, if you've actually started, show in the action plan what stage you've reached. Give yourselves time to do the job properly which, in the long run, will ensure you 'do' inclusion well.

If you're starting out to write your first SEN policy, you may be wondering whether you should write the policy and then use it in your working practices, or work out which practices suit your children and the setting best and then write the policy from that. The reality is that this concept of policy/practice is actually an unbroken circle – your good practice should influence your policy, and your policy should enable good practice to continue and develop.

Figure 2.1	The policy/practice issue – an unbroken circle

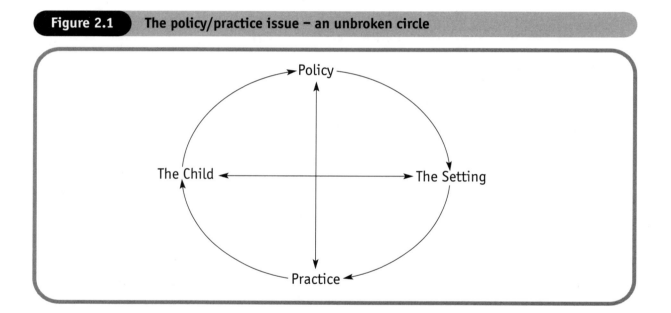

Don't re-invent your setting's wheel. Look at what you're doing now with regard to the children who have SEN. You're almost certainly differentiating their work and activities; my guess is you'll have allocated a key worker to them; you'll be keeping careful records and continually monitoring their progress; you'll have a good system of communication with their parents and you'll be thinking 'Where next?' It's a safe bet that much of what goes into an SEN policy is already happening in your daily routine. When you read the section below, *What needs to go into an inclusive SEN policy?*, establish which things you're already doing. You'll probably be pleasantly surprised that in fact you're well on the way to having the framework of your policy already done. So let the policy lead the practice and the practice lead the policy – and don't lose sleep over the process!

THE DIFFERENCE BETWEEN INCLUSION AND INTEGRATION

Inclusion is now automatically part of the planning in early years settings, but you may still hear people referring to 'integration'. The two terms are often used interchangeably but they do not mean the same thing. 'Integration' was the buzz-word after the SEN legislation of 1981, and mainstream schools began integrating children with special needs into their settings. Over time, though, there's been a gradual change in how we best support children with SEN, and the concept of inclusion has developed from this, the term itself coming into more regular use from about 1996.

So what is the difference between inclusion and integration? Let's have a look.

- *Integration* means having children with special educational needs in a main-stream setting and expecting them to change in order to 'fit in'. Their disability or difficulty is seen as coming from within the child and needing to be cured or corrected by remedial means. Integration doesn't encourage or make possible any changes in the setting, whether of attitudes or practices by its staff, so that the child can join in all activities as fully as possible. In other words, *the onus is on the child to change*. This is known as the medical model of the child and their difficulties.

- *Inclusion* means having children with special educational needs in a main-stream setting and making sure the setting's attitudes, policies and practices change and adapt so that the child can join in as fully as possible. In other words, *the onus is on the setting and everybody involved in it to change, if necessary*. The child's disabilities or difficulties are seen as part of the whole picture. This is known as the social model of the child and their difficulties.

It's an important distinction and as SENCO for your setting or cluster, you're in a superb position to spread the word and make sure that everybody understands the difference between the two concepts and uses the correct terminology.

POLICIES AS WORKING DOCUMENTS, CONSTANTLY UNDER REVIEW

As we've seen, the policy is definitely not a document to quickly download from computer software, ready for next week's *Ofsted* inspection and then to be dumped in the back of a filing cabinet. It's your key to including all children in your setting and it's a framework on which to develop your SEN provision. In other words, it's a **working document** produced by your setting to let everybody know what your aims are with regard to the children in your care. It should be constantly changing and being adapted to suit your needs at any particular point in time, and constantly being challenged, questioned and analysed for its effectiveness. It isn't a 'one size fits all' document, written and then left, but a well-used reference for developing and recording the good practice that goes on in your setting. So keep tweaking it to make it work!

THE ROLE OF THE SENCO IN POLICY DEVELOPMENT AND IMPLEMENTATION

Maybe you've never written a policy before and you're feeling panic at the very thought of it. If you are, but, as the SENCO, you can't avoid the issue, take heart – nobody in the setting can run away from it, or dump it all on you, because policymaking is a joint effort. The important thing is not to see it as an awesome task, an obligation, a useless exercise, or just something to keep the *Ofsted* inspector quiet. A carefully planned, well-written SEN policy will, in the long run, save you a great deal of time and it will ensure that the little ones in your care receive the support and the enjoyable experience of early years education that they're entitled to.

Your role is **to see to the day-to-day operation of the policy,** and how you do this will be explored in the relevant chapters of this book. But if you're starting from scratch, your main task is to organise the practicalities of getting people together to do the planning, discussing and writing up. There's more about how to do this later. Remember – you're not on your own and you can get help, support and advice from various people.

As we saw earlier, it's likely that writing your SEN policy is going to be a question of recording the things you're already doing. While you, as SENCO, will see to the daily operation of the policy, it is, in fact, a total ownership thing – everybody should make sure it's being acted on wherever they can. It's only by actually working with the policy that its strengths and weaknesses will be highlighted, so all 'chalk-face workers' must continually think about where the policy works well and where it's becoming a pain, for whatever reason. It's important you encourage them to tell you what they have discovered for the next policy review.

WHAT NEEDS TO GO INTO AN INCLUSIVE SEN POLICY?

The *SEN Code of Practice* suggests what you need to include and among the most important are the following:

- *Information about the aims and objectives of the policy.* Ask yourselves, 'What are our aims in the policy we're drawing up?' 'Are we aiming for inclusion of children with different needs?' 'Does our policy make sure that happens?'

- *The name of the SENCO and any specialities offered by members of staff.* Give the name of any practitioner within the setting who has a qualification and/or training in any field of SEN, and what their speciality is. For example,

'Our Manager, Anne Jones, holds an M.Ed. and has specialised in working with children who have autism'.

● *The arrangements for provision for children who have special educational needs.* Ask yourselves, 'How are we going to support children with different needs in terms of resources, staffing, time and so on?' Look at how the setting's organised, run, staffed and equipped, reviewing these and making sure each element includes children with additional needs, adapting them if necessary. Keep this in general terms because you can't possibly plan for every kind of additional need or condition. The 'tailor-made' provision will come when you're admitting a child with an identified difficulty and you plan their Individual Education Plan (IEP).

● *The arrangements for admission of children with special educational needs.* Agree your approach to admitting children with additional needs – for example, whether you'll have a transition or familiarisation period, whether you'll invite parents to stay with the child initially, whether it will be necessary to make some adaptations within the setting and so on.

● *The arrangements for identifying and assessing special educational needs.* The yardstick you use for identification and assessment has to be outlined in the policy. Ask yourselves, *Who will do it? When? Where? How?* For example, will it be done by the child's own key practitioner, the SENCO, the manager/head? Will it be done at a set time, or a time when the assessor happens to be 'free' to do it? Will it be done in your normal daily activity sessions or as a designated assessment/observation session? What form will they take – will you use the Foundation Stage profile, standardised assessments, observations (and what type of observation?) and so on?

● *The arrangements for providing access for children with special educational needs to a balanced and broadly based curriculum.* Ask yourselves how you'll ensure that all the children, regardless of ability or the difficulties being experienced, have the opportunities and experiences of the full curriculum on offer, whether this is the Foundation Stage or the National Curriculum. Review your resources and how you use them, whether the equipment, games and activities can be effectively and appropriately used by children with differing needs. It may mean adjusting the timetable, the venue, the staffing, etc. to enable the children with additional needs to access everything that's on offer. Review how you plan and implement IEPs making sure that your procedures do actually result in effective support for each child.

● *The procedures for reviewing the needs of a child with special educational needs.* When, where and how will reviews be carried out? Who will be involved? The *SEN Code of Practice* offers suggestions, but some things are unique to each setting. Because you have to consider your own facilities – timetable, staffing, clientele, and so on – in the decision making, your agreed arrangements will be unique.

● *The partnership with parents and other establishments or agencies.* This includes parents' access to Parent Partnership Services (PPS) and/or Independent Parental Support Services (IPSSs). Do you have procedures for making sure parents are made aware of their rights? Do you have arrangements in place for parents who don't speak English or who have alternative communication systems themselves such as sign language? Examine your links with other establishments such as schools, childminding networks and other early years settings – who are they with and how are they maintained? Ask yourselves, too, whether the links help with the inclusion of all children. And don't forget links with other outside agencies such as social services, health, education welfare services and voluntary organisations. How are your links with these maintained? Look at your arrangements for staff training in the area of SEN – how will you make sure staff can access it? Your Early Years Development and Childcare Partnership (EYDCP) or Sure Start scheme, and Local Education Authority (LEA) will offer this either in terms of in-house training, or information and advice about accessing training offered by other providers. (NB: at the time of writing, many EYDCPs were in the process of being phased out, but others were still active in many areas.) It's up to you as SENCO to make sure you can all tap into this source when you need to.

● *The criteria for evaluating the success of the SEN policy.* Ask yourselves when and how the policy will be reviewed, how everybody will decide its strengths and weaknesses and how you'll make any required changes. As the policy is used on a daily basis, its weaknesses will become apparent, how serious these are and how quickly they need to be addressed. Again, there isn't a blueprint because each setting is individual.

Some professionals advocate that a policy (any policy) should be no longer than one side of A4 paper. It's debatable whether those professionals have actually tried doing that, unless they used 8-point font and single spacing, written both horizontally and vertically on both sides of the page! However, if you feel that your policy is turning out to be a bit long, you can shorten it. Leave out the fine details that are in the main policy, and offer a condensed version for anybody who'd prefer one. If the full version is requested and/or needed, you can issue or use it then, as appropriate. The full version would be made available to *Ofsted* inspectors or perhaps parents who are going to be involved in IEP planning for their child who has additional needs, while the condensed version may be made available to people who don't, at that point, want the full text. As long as you make sure everybody knows that the complete version is available whenever they want it, you will have met the needs of all concerned. Don't forget to consider whether you will need copies of the policy translated into other languages. If you do, make sure that the translation is of a high standard and accurate. You'll find examples of both a shortened and a full-length SEN policy at the end of the chapter (pages 19–22).

PLANNING AND IMPLEMENTING AN INCLUSIVE SEN POLICY – SOME PRACTICAL IDEAS

The *SEN Code of Practice* requires everybody involved with your setting to write an inclusive SEN policy **together**, to publish it and make it available for anybody who's interested. As we have seen, you should plan and write the policy with the concept of inclusion running through it. Here's a summary of how the policy itself is actually everybody's baby:

- Its *management* is the manager's or head's responsibility.

- Its *planning, writing* and *publishing* is done by everybody appropriately involved with your setting.

- Its day-to-day *operation* is your responsibility, as the SENCO.

- Its *implementation* is the responsibility of you and all your colleagues within their own area.

So where on earth do I start? you might be asking. Never fear – once again, the answer lies in the planning, and in giving yourself and your colleagues time to do the job properly. Like Rome, a good policy isn't created in a day! Realistically, you'll need several meetings to agree and write it, and it'll be at least eight or nine months after you've put it into practice (or put your practices down on paper – which comes first?) and had a good few tweaks and revisions before you begin to see its strengths and weaknesses.

But let's assume you haven't yet done anything about your SEN policy. Here are some suggestions to get the process started:

- Arrange a meeting of everybody involved in your setting, including parents and, if required, outside agencies who could make a useful contribution to the discussion. (You can get the children's feedback during contact time.) As the SENCO, you're the person most likely to be in touch with everybody who should be involved.

- Before the meeting, send around copies of any LEA or setting management documentation that's relevant to SEN policies. This helps to focus people's minds and gives them a chance to note down anything they want to ask, comment on or discuss.

- If you can, designate a Chair and another person to take the minutes – don't do both of these yourself, as you need to be on the ball for making suggestions and answering queries. The Chair should be somebody who can keep the discussion focused and guided.

- Work through each section of the proposed policy, discussing it thoroughly. You're unlikely to crack it in one meeting, so be prepared for another couple of sessions before you're all happy with the draft.

- Ask for a volunteer to write the draft document, unless you have time to do it yourself.

- Before finishing the meeting, book the date of the next one while you have people captured!

- Include everything in the draft that was agreed at the meeting(s). Circulate copies of it to everybody involved, before the next meeting. This helps to refresh people's memories and gives them a chance to prepare their questions and queries, saving time in the meeting itself.

- Hold a meeting to finalise and approve the policy document. Agree how you'll get the policy to the parents and other interested parties. You may also have to consider the need for a translated version for people who don't speak English or who have alternative communication systems, and how you'll get the document to people who don't or can't come to the setting very often.

- Agree a start-date for the policy and book its first review meeting in about a term or three months, so it has a chance to pan out and you can see how it's beginning to work in practice.

- At the policy review meeting, especially if this is the first SEN policy that you've written, be prepared to make changes. Don't be afraid to do this. A policy is a working document and only by using it in practice will its strengths and weaknesses be highlighted. There'll be some things you want to change, but also some things that are so good you'll want them to remain.

- Agree any changes and issue the revised policy to everybody as soon as possible, then get the revised policy into practice immediately and keep monitoring the changes to make sure that they're doing what you wanted them to do.

AN EXAMPLE OF AN INCLUSIVE SEN POLICY (SHORT VERSION)

Dales View Nursery SEN Policy

We believe that all children, regardless of their individual needs, have the right to a broad, balanced and purposeful early years curriculum, and full access to all activities. Our intention is to **welcome** *all* children to an inclusive setting. In order to achieve this, **we aim** to identify any difficulties a child might have and to work closely with the children, their parents or carers and other agencies if this is necessary.

We admit all children living in the Dales View and Allen Valley Borough, aged 2 years 6 months to school age. Sometimes a child may need extra support in some way – **we encourage** parents who think their child might have particular needs to talk to us about this as soon as possible.

Our SENCO is Sarah Ellis and she helps everybody involved with our nursery in all aspects of supporting children with special educational needs and their families.

Sarah has completed the LEA's accredited course in supporting children with special educational needs. She attends six days' SEN training each year and she also meets other SENCOs regularly to share ideas and up-to-date information about SEN.

Anne Jones, our Nursery Manager, is also a trained and qualified speech and language therapist.

Our aim is to

- ensure a happy, caring and secure environment for everybody who works in or visits Dales View Nursery;

- ensure that everybody in our setting, their opinions and their talents are respected and valued;

- identify children's special educational needs as early as possible, and to work together with their parents to plan ways of supporting the children in managing their difficulties;

- differentiate, adapt and accommodate our curriculum, activities and materials when necessary, to ensure the inclusion of children with special educational needs;

- ensure that our plans for each child with special educational needs are appropriate;

- review at least once a month, with parents, their child's action plan(s) and make appropriate changes when necessary;

- acknowledge when we cannot meet the child's needs in Dales View Nursery and to discuss with their parents the request for support from outside professionals (no outside professional will be contacted without the parents' permission);

- work together with the outside professionals, the child and the parents to plan and use appropriately revised Individual Education Plans (IEPs) to support the child;

- acknowledge when we continue to be unable to meet the child's needs in Dales View Nursery, and to discuss with everybody involved, especially the parents, a request of the LEA for a statutory assessment of the child;

- review this policy every nine months and make any appropriate changes to ensure it is relevant to our setting and the children we care for.

Complaints about our SEN provision: If parents or carers have a complaint about the way we are working with their child who has SEN, they should speak to the key worker initially, and if they are still not happy, they should approach the SENCO (Sarah Ellis). She will look into the problem and report back within a week. If parents or carers continue to be dissatisfied, the SENCO will refer the matter to the Manager to take further action as appropriate.

AN EXAMPLE OF AN EARLY YEARS INCLUSIVE SEN POLICY (FULL-LENGTH VERSION)

Dales View Nursery SEN Policy

We believe that all children, regardless of their individual needs, have the right to a broad, balanced and purposeful early years curriculum, and full access to all activities. Our intention is to **welcome** *all* children to an inclusive setting. In order to achieve this, **we aim** to identify any difficulties a child might have and to work closely with the children, their parents or carers and other agencies if this is necessary.

We admit all children living in the Dales View and Allen Valley Borough, aged 2 years 6 months to school age. Sometimes a child may need extra support in some way – **we encourage** parents who think their child might have particular needs to talk to us about this as soon as possible.

Our SENCO is Sarah Ellis and she

- helps us to identify children's special educational needs;

- helps us with planning approaches to working with and supporting children with special educational needs;

- updates the parents with their children's progress;

- makes sure the children's progress is regularly reviewed;

- makes sure the parents are fully involved with the planning for their child.

Sarah has completed the LEA's accredited course in supporting children with special educational needs. Sarah attends six days' SEN training each year and she also meets other SENCOs regularly to share ideas and up-to-date information about SEN.

Anne Jones, our Nursery Manager, is also a trained and qualified speech and language therapist.

We have a wide selection of books and pamphlets about SEN and the LEA's support services for parents or carers to borrow – feel free to ask your child's key worker about these.

We have regular contact with the area physiotherapist and occupational therapist services.

Our buildings are suitable for wheelchair access and there is a loop system for the deaf and hard of hearing. We have purpose-built toilet and shower facilities for the disabled and also a quiet area. We have a soft-play room and the outdoor play area has been fitted with soft safety paving.

Our aim is to

- ensure a happy, caring and secure environment for everybody who works in or visits Dales View Nursery;

- ensure that everybody in our setting, their opinions and their talents are respected and valued;

- admit children with special educational needs after a familiarisation period which is appropriate to the child's needs; parents may stay with the child initially, according to the needs of the child;

- identify children's special educational needs as early as possible, using a variety of observations, assessments and monitoring procedures, according to the child's needs; assessments and identification of special educational needs will be done by the appropriate member(s) of staff; parents will be involved with and informed of each assessment;

- work together with parents to plan ways of supporting the children in managing their difficulties, deciding on programmes or plans of action according to each child's needs;

- differentiate, adapt and accommodate our curriculum, activities and materials when necessary, to ensure the inclusion of children with special educational needs; any adaptations will be made according to the needs of the child;

- ensure that our plans for each child with special educational needs are appropriate, closely monitoring their progress to make sure that the plans remain appropriate and relevant;

- review at least once a month, with parents, their child's action plan(s) and make appropriate changes when necessary;

- emphasise and encourage positive behaviour by everybody in the setting; this includes adults as well as children;

- acknowledge when we cannot meet the child's needs in Dales View Nursery and to discuss with their parents the request for support from outside professionals (no outside professional will be contacted without the parents' permission);

- work together with the outside professionals, the child and the parents to plan and use appropriately revised Individual Education Plans (IEPs) to support the child;

- regularly review the IEPs to ensure that they remain appropriate and effective for the child's progress;

- acknowledge when we continue to be unable to meet the child's needs in Dales View Nursery, and to discuss with everybody involved, especially the parents, a request of the LEA for a statutory assessment of the child;

- review this policy every nine months and make any appropriate changes to ensure it is relevant to our setting and the children we care for.

Complaints about our SEN provision: If parents or carers have a complaint about the way we are working with their child who has SEN, they should speak to the key worker initially, and if they are still not happy, they should approach the SENCO (Sarah Ellis). She will look into the problem and report back within a week. If parents or carers continue to be dissatisfied, the SENCO will refer the matter to the Manager to take further action as appropriate.

If you prefer different terminology from 'special educational needs', you could use phrases such as 'differing needs', 'different needs' or 'additional needs', to give you a few examples. Whichever phraseology you choose is, of course, a matter of personal choice for your setting and its circumstances, but above all, for the children in your care and their parents.

SUMMARY

The **key points** covered in this chapter were:

- The policy/practice issue – which comes first?
- The difference between inclusion and integration.
- Policies as working documents, constantly under review.
- The role of the SENCO in policy development and implementation.
- What needs to go into an inclusive SEN policy?
- Planning and implementing an SEN policy – some practical ideas.

Chapter 3

Supporting colleagues – giving help where it's needed

The **key points** covered in this chapter are:

- Support for the SENCO.
- The role of the SENCO in supporting colleagues.
- Practical ways of supporting colleagues.
- Delivering in-house special educational needs (SEN) training.

INTRODUCTION

If you're a new SENCO, you're possibly feeling a bit overwhelmed and unsure of what to do. This chapter explores some of the issues that may arise when you're considering how you can best tackle the role. It's important that you know where to go for support for yourself, since you must have this in order to effectively support your colleagues. The most important thing to remember is that **you don't have to do it all yourself**, but you must let everybody know this. The people of the north east of England have a lovely saying that sums it all up:

Shy bairns get nowt.

There's plenty of help around, so find out where it is, and ask for it!

SUPPORT FOR THE SENCO

If you haven't looked at the self-posed questions in Chapter 1 (page 2), now might be a good time to go back and have a little ponder. It's vital that you're comfortable and confident in your role as SENCO, since an unhappy professional won't be as effective as one who's clear about their way forward. Before you're in a strong position to support your colleagues, you'll need to ensure your own needs and requirements are met. Examine your level of knowledge and expertise, and/or confidence in the field of additional needs. Ask yourself whether you're able to demonstrate to colleagues your:

- commitment to and good practice of inclusion;

- management and organisation of resources, personnel and time (your own as well as others');

- knowledge of effective teaching strategies and techniques;

- ability to analyse and exploit children's learning styles;

- ability to identify children's additional needs and plan effective ways to support them;

- knowledge of SEN legislation, recent research and information;

- leadership and decision-making abilities;

- communication and cooperative skills.

You may well think of other areas not on this list that you'd like to develop or refine. When you've identified your needs, liaise with your manager or head to explore ways of fulfilling them.

During this process, it's easy to lose confidence in yourself and begin to believe you can't do the job. Try not to fall into this trap, because you *can* do the job. Here are a few fundamentals to remember.

It's vitally important that you:

- recognise and feel confident about your expertise, experience and abilities – you wouldn't be in the job if you weren't capable of doing it;

- don't feel deskilled because of an impression that you have to be all things to all people – it's a false impression, and deskilled is the last thing you are;

- recognise and accept your limitations, however, and then do something about it – nobody will think less of you for asking for help, quite the reverse;

- link up with any SENCO group or network that meets in your locality – this will give you a source of ideas, help and support, information, and somewhere to find out what's available that may be useful;

- let your manager or head know of anything happening within your setting that you're uneasy about – children with additional needs are the most vulnerable little ones in your care, and if any element in the setting adds to that vulnerability, you must act to stop it;

● remember that your colleagues should support you, as well as the other way around – they can make helping the child much more effective by playing their part to the full, including giving you support too, so ask for it.

If you're working from a non-school setting (e.g. playgroup, childminding network, Early Years Development and Childcare Partnership [EYDCP] or Sure Start, etc.) always have your Area SENCO's phone number near to hand as they're almost sure to be your first point of contact for help. Even if they can't provide it personally, they'll be able to point you in the right direction. Link in with your local primary schools which can give you another strand of resources, help and support.

The *SEN Code of Practice* acknowledges that to do the job effectively, the SENCO needs to have time allocated for SEN work, and suggests that the SENCO should be a member of the senior management team. This may be difficult to achieve in a non-maintained setting or a widely scattered situation such as a childminding network. If you're finding time a problem, discuss the situation with your line manager and point out what the difficulties are. Explore ways of addressing the problem, e.g. delegating some of the paperwork, reducing other commitments, allocating some non-contact time, etc. Time management and paperwork are recognised difficulties within the job, and you must exploit every opportunity to address these.

THE ROLE OF THE SENCO IN SUPPORTING COLLEAGUES

The *SEN Code of Practice* states that part of the SENCO's role is to advise and support the other practitioners in the setting. Defining here how to do this would be a bit like asking how long a piece of string is. The quality, type, and quantity of support depend very much on each setting's situation, and even then will change from year to year.

If you're starting out to assess what your colleagues' needs are, your first course of action should be to ask them. Your perception of what they need (and/or want) may be very different from theirs. Again, how you go about this will depend on your setting. Maybe you can draw up a list of needs during a conversation over a cup of coffee with your colleagues, or maybe you rarely have the chance for such an informal get-together so need a different way of gathering the information, e.g. distributing a questionnaire.

However you glean your answers, the following list may help to focus thoughts (yours and/or your colleagues') when assessing professional needs within your setting.

Consider whether any colleague needs help to:

- understand the concept of inclusion (not integration) and how to practise it;

- identify children with additional needs;

- appropriately assess children with additional needs;

- take part in planning differentiated work and activities for the child;

- formulate Individual Education Plans (IEPs);

- monitor the effectiveness of the IEPs and adjust them if appropriate;

- devise effective strategies and techniques for working with children who have difficulties with their
  - communication and interaction
  - cognition and learning
  - behavioural, emotional and social development
  - sensory and/or physical development;

- prepare for and take part in IEP reviews;

- understand the processes behind Early Years Action, Early Years Action Plus and Statutory Assessment;

- work with the child's parents;

- work with outside agencies;

- work with colleagues within the setting.

Once you have your feedback, discuss with your manager or head ways of addressing the issues raised by your colleagues.

PRACTICAL WAYS OF SUPPORTING COLLEAGUES

Let's look at some strategies for offering support to your colleagues. You may need to peel back the institutional layers and review your setting from the bottom up (or even the top down!), to see where it supports the staff, and therefore offers effective support for the children.

The curriculum

Have a look at the curriculum you're offering, whether this is under the banner of standardised curricula (Foundation Stage and/or National Curriculum) or from a particular philosophy or practice, and decide whether it's truly inclusive. Children with additional needs will be effectively supported within your setting only if your curriculum:

- is regularly reviewed;

- is well planned;

- is well organised;

- facilitates the learning styles and needs of the children;

- accommodates the teaching styles and all-round skills of the practitioners;

- is constantly evaluated and monitored;

- is adjusted where it fails to address the needs of the children.

When, as a staff, you're planning work, sessions, activities, etc. these curriculum characteristics may help you to focus on the curriculum and ask yourselves, *Is it working?*

Support within the working areas

You should explore the type, extent and level of support for practitioners within the working areas, at the chalk face so to speak. There are many ways of providing this, again depending on your particular situation, and the specific needs of any given child. These can include:

- Differentiated Learning Plans (DLPs), IEPs or Statements of Special Educational Needs – the roadmaps towards enabling the child to develop and progress;

- specific teaching and/or management techniques;

- an allocated Learning Support Assistant (LSA) or Teaching Assistant (TA);

- support from an outside agent working with the child and/or the key practitioner;

- time allocated for working with the child, either on a one-to-one basis or within a group (i.e. the rest of the children are handed over to another practitioner);

- adapted resources and/or furniture;

- specialised equipment.

Discussing these issues with the key worker will enable you to decide together what's the most effective method of supporting them. By encouraging your colleague to share with you their requirements, you'll be better placed to ensure they receive the help they feel they need.

Outside links

You can access support for yourself and/or your colleagues by developing and maintaining links with a number of organisations or bodies outside your setting. Doing this will give you an opening to:

- information

- people

- services

all of which offer support in a variety of ways.

If you're in a non-school setting, establish links with your local primary/first/infant school, and make sure you maintain those links: suggest regular meetings or get-togethers, ask whether their SENCO would be willing to share ideas and expertise with you on a two-way basis, invite their staff for the occasional social 'do', offer to share your early years resources or equipment or facilities, etc. Setting up such links and sharing best practice ensures a standardised and seamless provision for all the children in your area, as well as providing a source of support and help for the practitioners involved.

Make sure your colleagues know that support and advice is available from your local authority support services. What they will offer you depends on the need you identify within the setting. There's a fuller discussion of this in Chapter 7, which explores the services and their role.

Always remember that your Area SENCO is there as the first port of call, as are your Sure Start team and/or EYDCP. If they can't provide the support you need directly, they'll certainly know where you can get it, and will put you in touch with the appropriate organisation.

Enabling colleagues to practise inclusion

Practising inclusion doesn't mean you have to get 'Mickey the Brickie' in tomorrow to widen your doors and fit a lift. Fine if that's appropriate for your building, but the reality of inclusion is more complex and more subtle, and probably also much easier than turning your working areas into a building site.

As a staff, review your setting together.

- Reassess your furniture to see whether it's suitable for children with, for example, physical problems or sensory difficulties. (If you don't have a child at the moment with such difficulties, this can be left until an appropriate time.)

- Get some adjustable tables, or a selection of different height surfaces.

- Place tables near natural light, or good quality artificial light.

- Make sure that chairs are the right height for a correct posture.

- Have some chairs with arms to support the child in a secure sitting position.

- Make spaces between tables and other pieces of furniture to avoid collisions when the children are moving around the room.

- Keep furniture and designated areas in the same place.

- Keep the layout of apparatus the same.

- Don't have polished floors, so giving a more secure foothold and preventing light reflection.

- Keep the floor clear of small items such as pencils, building blocks and so on.

- Have doors that open and close easily, but don't swing back to nip fingers.

- Make sure everybody keeps cupboard doors and drawers closed.

- If you have steps, fit handrails and/or ramps if necessary. (You can include this in your medium-term planning for redecorating and refurbishment of the setting if there aren't any children in the setting who require handrails or ramps.)

- Make sure the toilets and hand basins are accessible.

- Have a quiet area available at all times. This must be regarded as a pleasant place where the child can go to 'wind down' – it must never be used as a 'sin bin' or punishment.

- Display pictures, labels and captions, etc. at the lowest child's height.

- Cover sharp and/or extruding corners with foam.

Have a look at your resources, books and equipment.

- Ensure the child who works at floor level has access to the sand and water play by putting the trays on the floor. It's also a fun experience for the able-bodied children, and by all playing together, the children are fully included.

- Use big cushions or beanbags to support the child who works and/or plays at floor level.

- Keep easels and stands in good repair and check they're steady and secure.

- Use jumbo size paintbrushes and crayons, etc. or wrap standard sized handles in foam rubber for the child who has difficulty holding them.

- Exploit all the child's senses in sand or water play by putting colours and/or scents into sand or water.

- Have some musical instruments that vibrate and others that don't need vision to play. If you have a wooden floor make it vibrate by stamping or thumping on it. Let the children feel the vibrations with their bare feet or their cheeks.

- Have easy-to-find-and-use door and drawer handles – if you can, have knobs.

- Use Dycem® mats (or similar) to secure small equipment on surfaces.

- Have some persona dolls and books to explore the concept of disability and to develop a positive image of people who have additional needs.

- During story time, circle time or group discussions, use dolls with aids such as glasses, callipers or a hearing aid, as part of the session.

- Have books with clear, bold images and pictures.

- Read books and stories that feature characters with a disability, but not necessarily as the main character.

- Store books and equipment on shelves that are at child-friendly height.

- Use tactile materials such as sandpaper, velvet, polystyrene or bubble wrap to make labels, cards, etc.

- Use a variety of balls for catching and throwing games, e.g. with a bell inside, with different surfaces (such as smooth rubber or tennis balls), of different weights, that move erratically, with different smells made by soaking tennis balls in different scents.

- Make sure both the small play-equipment and the outdoor equipment is accessible.

Encourage your colleagues to:

- allocate a key worker to the child;

- speak positively to the child – e.g. 'Come and sit with me, Jaspal, and we'll share this book' would be more effective than 'Sit down and stop doing that, Jaspal';

- speak facing the child so that they get the whole message without losing either its beginning or its end;

- always have a relaxed and warm facial expression;

- attract the child's attention by gently touching their shoulder and saying their name before speaking (but you need to be aware of whether the child will tolerate this and/or, where appropriate, bear safety and legal issues/implications in mind);

- give instructions in small, easy-to-digest 'bite-size' amounts, if necessary one step at a time;

- keep to the daily routine as much as possible;

- help the child to achieve their targets using games and other play-based activities;

- watch for any personality clashes (whether child–practitioner or child–child) and if necessary change the routine to avoid difficult situations;

- maintain a positive and mutually supportive relationship with the child's parents;

- learn to use equipment, communication systems or other special facilities that the child may have.

You can find a useful framework for developing inclusive practices in *Index for Inclusion: Developing Learning and Participation in Schools*,[1] a publication of the Centre for Studies on Inclusive Education (2000). The *Index* was circulated to all LEAs, primary, secondary and special schools and should be available from your LEA.

In-service training

As SENCO, one of your main roles is to ensure you and your colleagues can access appropriate and effective in-service training (INSET) in the field of additional needs. How you achieve this obviously depends on your situation and circumstances. SENCOs from childminding networks, playgroups or out-of-school clubs, for example, are more likely to receive training in cluster groups, provided by the LEA, Sure Start team or other authority, mainly because this is the most effective way to organise it – a playgroup based in a village hall, meeting twice a week, isn't likely to be in a position to deliver in-house INSET. On the other hand, a SENCO with a specialist qualification in a large primary school could deliver INSET within their school, inviting colleagues from link establishments to join them.

Whatever your situation, it's crucial that the training you obtain for your colleagues and/or yourself is of the highest quality, and is effective in terms of enabling effective SEN support. Finance will of course be a factor you have to take into account, but as with all things, training on the cheap may cost you dear in the end. Commission the best you can afford, ensuring it's delivered by a professional with both qualifications and expertise in the field, but also (crucially, I would argue) one who delivers the training in an interesting, practical and vibrant way. You want to come back from training inspired and enthused, as well as knowledgeable – a day with a provider who bores you out of your box won't ensure that!

You may find it useful to think about your setting from the inside out – whether you can access in-house training, what type of training is needed, how much, for how long and by whom. Ask yourself:

- whether there's somebody on the staff with a specialist qualification who can deliver some training;
- what the training needs of your colleagues are;
- what's the most urgent type of SEN training required by the majority of the staff, e.g. challenging behaviour, learning difficulties, language and communication difficulties, practising inclusion, etc. – prioritise these and organise the training as and when you can afford it;
- what are the requirements of the children with additional needs in terms of expertise by the staff supporting them;

Figure 3.1   **An example of a typical Course Evaluation Form**

COURSE EVALUATION

Course title: _____

To what extent did the course meet its objectives?

Please comment on the process of the course: e.g. the presentation, the activities, the balance of activities.

If you were running the course, is there anything you might add or omit?

REFLECTION AND ACTION PLANNING

In what ways do you think the children could benefit from your attendance at this course?

What could you/the setting do to ensure they get the benefits?

What could be the steps to achieving that?

- how to allocate training places on a 'needs first' basis;

- where you can get funding for the training;

- whether there are outside sources of extra funding for training (ask your Area SENCO).

Once you've spent precious finances on training, it's vital you evaluate what happened and whether you had value for money. Most authorities, establishments and training providers issue evaluation sheets to training participants, so ask for copies of these to help with your evaluation. The feedback will help you to make an informed decision about future training plans. Figure 3.1 shows a typical Evaluation Form.

From the overall opinion of the participants, you'll be able to judge whether your money was well spent, whether you'd commission that provider/trainer again, whether the training can be effectively be put into practice in your setting, whether you can share and/or cascade the training for wider benefit, and so on.

Depending on the size of your setting, you might choose to keep a record of who's received what training, when, etc. Figure 3.2 illustrates the type of Summary Form you could use for this. There's a blank photocopiable version of the form on page 58.

A Summary Form such as this can prove very useful for ensuring a fair distribution of training opportunities across the staff, a balanced choice of training courses so that all areas requiring development are addressed, and value for money is achieved. You can also see whether a picture builds up of any single provider receiving consistently poor or consistently positive evaluations, so helping you to make informed choices in your future planning.

DELIVERING IN-HOUSE SEN TRAINING

If you find that you're 'It' in your setting (i.e. the designated trainer), rather than buying in the training, you may find the materials in this section to be of use. It's a mini-course that you can adapt to suit yourself, or use as it stands. The sheets can be photocopied for handouts or to make overhead transparencies, or you could design a PowerPoint presentation if you and your computer are an item.

Figure 3.2   **Record of Staff SEN Training**

Name	Date of training	Course attended	Purpose of course	Provider	Value (scale 1–10)
Ann Scott	12.11.04	SEN Code of Practice in Practice	Principles of using CoP	Adam Smith Training Associates	10 – excellent day
May Howard	12/19/26 Jan. 05 & 2 Feb. 05	Managing Challenging Behaviour in the Early Years	Strategies to work with children with EBD	Hamptonshire LEA EBD Support Service	5 – average content; poor delivery
Don Smith	15.01.05	Role of the SENCO	SENCO training	Hamptonshire LEA SEN Support Service	9 – good delivery; good content
Ann Scott	13/20/27 Feb. 05	Lang. Lit. & Comm. for EY Children with SEN	Strategies for teaching language & literacy skills	Hamptonshire LEA Literacy Advisers & University of Hamptonshire	8 – very useful; good content; delivery so-so

SUMMARY

The **key points** covered in this chapter were:

- Support for the SENCO.

- The role of the SENCO in supporting colleagues.

- Practical ways of supporting colleagues.

- Delivering in-house SEN training.

References

1 *Index for Inclusion: Developing Learning and Participation in Schools* by T. Booth, M. Ainscow, K. Black-Hawkins, M. Vaughan and L. Shaw (Centre for Studies on Inclusive Education, 2000; see Further reading for details of how to obtain a copy).

1. The Special Educational Needs Code of Practice

The *Special Educational Needs (SEN) Code of Practice* provides for

- the inclusion of children in **all** Early Years provision

- the involvement of both the child and the parents in all procedures

- the right of appeal for parents

- Individual Education Plans (IEPs) that focus only on what is **additional to** and **different from** the rest of the curriculum.

Early Years Action involves

- identifying areas of concern

- planning, writing and implementing IEPs

- holding IEP reviews and planning the way forward.

Early Years Action Plus involves

- referring to and working with outside agents

- continually monitoring areas of progress and areas of concern

- writing and implementing more specialised IEPs

- holding IEP reviews and planning the way forward.

Statutory Assessment involves

- parents, maintained school or nursery school requesting the Local Education Authority (LEA) to make a statutory assessment of the child

- childminders or private nurseries bringing a child to the attention of the LEA, which then decides whether a statutory assessment is required.

- The Early Years provider must supply the LEA with all relevant records, and information and advice on health-related matters from the appropriate agents.

- When the LEA considers and assessment, it asks
  - what difficulties were identified by the provider
  - whether individualised teaching strategies were put in place
  - whether parental views have been considered
  - whether outside advice was obtained regarding the child's

physical health and function   **communication skills**
self-help skills   **perceptual and motor skills**
emotional and behavioural development   **social skills**
responses to learning experiences

A Statement of Special Educational Needs

- should take no longer than six months to be issued

- must be reviewed every six months if the child is under five years, or annually above that age.

© Collette Drifte, *A Manual for the Early Years SENCO*, Paul Chapman Publishing, 2005

Inclusion or integration – what's the difference?

- **Integration:** placing the child in a mainstream setting and expecting them to change and adapt in order to 'fit in'; integration fails to encourage or facilitate the changes in attitude necessary at institutional and individual levels, to enable the child to participate as fully as possible; *the onus is on the child to change.*

- **Inclusion:** placing the child in a mainstream setting and ensuring the attitudes, policies and practices at institutional and individual levels enable the child to participate as fully as possible; *the onus is on the setting and everybody involved in it to change, if necessary.*

What are the benefits of inclusion?

- Children with special educational needs (SEN) benefit from contact with all their peers and vice versa.

- Parents become fuller members of the community and are less isolated.

- Positive pre-school experiences mean that parents are more likely to choose mainstream primary schools for their children.

- Setting staff and other adults benefit from contact with children who have SEN.

- Good practice in the care and education of children with SEN can improve good practice for all the children in the setting.

(Adapted from *All Together: How to Create Inclusive Services for Disabled Children and Their Families. A Practical Handbook for Early Years Workers*, M. Dickins, and J. Denziloe, National Early Years Network, draft 2nd edn, 2002; National Children's Bureau, 2003)

ACTIVITY

Are the following scenarios examples of inclusive practice? If not, what strategies might the practitioners use to make sure the child is included? Discuss these with a partner.

1. **Andrew**, who is almost 4, has Attention Deficit Hyperactive Disorder (ADHD) and he takes the drug Ritalin. He goes to his local pre-school group and when he arrives, he runs wildly around the room crashing into the furniture and the other children. Some of the parents have complained and the practitioners have asked Andrew's parents to withdraw him from the group.

2. **Lucy** is 3. She goes to nursery every day and is dropped off very early by her mother on the way to work. Most afternoons, Lucy goes between activity areas pushing the other children or spoiling their games or work, usually ending up in tears. The practitioners discussed the problem with Lucy's Mum and decided to let Lucy have a sleep after lunch while the other children have Quiet Time, so that she's refreshed for the afternoon's activities.

3. **Melanie** is 4 and goes to playschool. She has problems working in large groups such as story time or discussions, usually disrupting the session with inappropriate behaviour. One of the practitioners takes Melanie for a one-to-one session in the library while the others have the group session so ensuring the other children's activity isn't ruined.

4. **Jason**, who is 3, always made a mess at snack time in his nursery, by taking biscuits off the plate and throwing them on the floor, and by tipping his beaker of juice all over the table. The practitioners decided to give him a drinking cup with a sealed lid. They also changed the system with the biscuits, by giving each child a turn (including Jason) at distributing them to the others.

Answers to Inclusion Activity

1. **Andrew**: this is not inclusion. The setting needs to show both the parents and the other children that there is nothing to fear from Andrew's difficulties. The practitioners need to encourage an ethos of welcoming all children, regardless of their difficulties, and to arrange the activities to enable Andrew to take part without provoking bouts of inappropriate behaviour. There should be close liaison with Andrew's parents and the relevant medical professionals to enable effective planning.

2. **Lucy**: this is inclusion. Lucy's practitioners have realised there's a pattern to her inappropriate behaviour – in the afternoons and probably because she's tired after a very early start. By adjusting Lucy's afternoon activities to take account of this (i.e. differentiating), the practitioners have ensured that she's included in the other things that are on offer.

3. **Melanie**: this is not inclusion. Melanie is being deprived of an activity that is on offer to the other children, and also of the chance to develop her speaking, listening, turn-taking and social skills. One practitioner could work with Melanie before the group session, explaining what it's going to be about and helping her to prepare her contribution. When Melanie becomes restless then the practitioner could withdraw her to the Library, but encouraging her over a period of time to stay with the group for longer.

4. **Jason**: this is inclusion. The practitioners realise that Jason has difficulty in managing the beaker and is probably a bit overwhelmed by all the biscuits on one plate. By giving him a cup that he can use more easily and by changing the biscuit routine, Jason is included in snack time without the previous stresses.

The role of the SENCO

The main responsibilities of the SENCO are

- to ensure liaison with the child's parents and other professionals who may be involved with the child

- to advise and support the other practitioners working in the setting

- to ensure that appropriate Individual Education Plans (IEPs) are being implemented

- to ensure that all relevant background information and records respecting the child are collected, recorded and kept up to date

- to ensure the setting's special educational needs (SEN) policy is implemented, monitored and reviewed, and updated when appropriate

The *SEN Code of Practice* recognises that time should be allocated to the SENCO for coordination.

The *SEN Code of Practice* suggests that the SENCO should be a member of the senior management team.

Early Years Action

The practitioner should

- identify the areas of difficulty

- discuss with the parents the involvement of the SENCO

- provide the SENCO with as much information as possible

- ask the parents about any other problems (e.g. health); observe the child

- maintain accurate and updated records of the child's progress

- liaise with the child's parents, the SENCO and the child to plan an Individual Education Plan (IEP)

- implement the IEP

- be involved in and attend the IEP review.

The SENCO should

- make sure the parents are completely involved and informed

- collect all known information about the child within the setting

- conduct and/or collect in-house assessments of the child and their progress

- decide with the practitioner and parents on the action to be taken, and plan the IEP

- ensure the continual monitoring of the effectiveness of the IEP

- ensure accurate and updated record keeping

- arrange a review meeting (at least once every three months).

Early Years Action Plus

The practitioner should

- collect all the relevant information on the child for the SENCO

- attend a review meeting with the child's parents and the SENCO to decide on the action to take

- plan a new Individual Education Plan (IEP) with the external specialist, the parents and the child

- implement the IEP

- maintain regular and careful record keeping

- if appropriate, involve the Learning Support Assistant in planning and record keeping

- be involved in and attend the next review.

The SENCO should

- request help from the appropriate outside specialist

- inform the child's parents of the Local Education Authority's Parent Partnership Service

- ensure all relevant records are updated and make them available to the external specialist

- make sure advice and support from external agents are available to both the early years professional and the child's parents

- work with the specialist agent(s), the child's Early Years professional, the child and parents to plan a new IEP, the targets, and the teaching strategies

- ensure the IEP is continually monitored for its effectiveness

- arrange an IEP review at least every three months/once per term inviting everybody concerned, including the child if possible.

Statutory Assessment and Statements of Special Educational Needs

The practitioner should

- collect all the relevant information on the child for the Local Education Authority (LEA)

- complete the report (Educational Advice) on the child's progress in response to the LEA's request for such advice

- liaise with the external specialist, the parents and the child

- continue to implement the current Individual Education Plan (IEP)

- maintain regular and careful record keeping

- if appropriate, involve Learning Support Assistant in planning and record keeping

- be involved in and attend the Annual or Biannual reviews.

The SENCO should

- collect all the relevant information on the child for the LEA including the Educational Advice, and forward it to the LEA

- continue to liaise with the relevant outside specialist(s)

- inform the child's parents of the LEA's Parent Partnership Service

- ensure all relevant records continue to be monitored and updated

- work with the specialist agent(s), the child's Early Years professional, the child and parents to continue the current IEP

- ensure the IEP is continually monitored for its effectiveness

- arrange the Annual or Biannual Review, or ensure the LEA arranges it.

At all levels (Early Years Action, Early Years Action Plus, Statutory Assessment and Statements and Special Educational Needs)

The parent/carer should be encouraged to

- agree to support their child at home through specified activities, targets, programmes, etc.

- liaise with the main practitioner and, if appropriate, the SENCO, to plan differentiated programmes of work, Individual Education Plans (IEPs), Play Plans, etc.

- offer all relevant information about their child that will help in planning effective support

- advise the key practitioner of any problems or difficulties at home that may affect the child's progress (in confidence)

- attend all reviews, meetings or discussions regarding their child

- liaise with outside professionals at Early Years Action Plus

- ensure their child has sufficient affection and love, has sufficient sleep, a balanced diet, is appropriately dressed according to the season, and attends the setting regularly.

The child should

- be involved (where possible and appropriate) in all discussions, plans and arrangements relevant to their support in the setting

- be helped to understand the reason for their IEPs

- be helped to understand their IEP targets and encouraged to achieve these

- be encouraged to go to their key worker for support, sympathy or any other reason, when they feel the need

- have access to a full, broad and balanced early years curriculum, and be fully included in all activities.

Communication and interaction

Watch for the little one who

- hardly ever talks or does not talk at all

- stammers or has slow speech, but understands what you say to them, and what they say makes sense

- has delayed or distorted speech that's difficult to understand

- has normal speech but what they say may be odd or inappropriate in context

- has normal speech but doesn't seem to understand what you say to them and/or doesn't respond appropriately to other people

- speaks at inappropriate times or makes inappropriate remarks

- laughs very loudly or for too long

- finds it hard to take turns during conversations and/or has poor conversational skills

- has ritualistic or obsessive behaviours or habits

- has problems communicating through speech and/or other forms of language

- can't use appropriate verbal and/or non-verbal language

- doesn't react 'normally' in social situations or avoids social situations

- behaves passively and has little or no initiative or curiosity

- seems to be unaware of other people and their needs or emotions

- has unusual voice tone, uses bizarre language and/or ritualistic phrases such as advertisement jingles or slogans.

Cognition and learning

Look out for the little one who

- has poor scores on assessments or profiles compared with the other children of the same age in their group

- has markedly lower levels of development (in all or specific areas) and play than those of the other children

- finds difficulty in developing their skills, especially in communication and interaction, literacy and numeracy

- can't deal with abstract ideas and/or generalise concepts from personal experience (older children)

- makes little or no progress in spite of involvement in the nursery curriculum

- doesn't achieve their set targets

- makes little or no progress despite your differentiated curriculum.

Behavioural, emotional and social development

Watch for the child who

- is verbally and/or physically aggressive with other children and/or adults

- is introverted or withdrawn, or seems troubled and worried

- is loud and inappropriately outgoing

- behaves inappropriately for their chronological age

- has strange or socially inappropriate behaviour

- does things that may cause self-injury

- can't stay on task, despite support and encouragement from an adult

- regularly disrupts the routine

- doesn't make progress

- is often absent

- has bouts of uncooperative behaviour

- behaves unpredictably and/or has erratic attitudes to learning

- shows little interest in activities and games

- seems to be over-dependent on adults

- seems to be hyperactive

- can't play with other children, or play with them 'normally'

- can't share or take turns with toys and equipment

- shows poor or no conversational skills.

Sensory and/or physical

See if the child

- has difficulty in coordinating their hands and feet

- experiences problems in balancing

- has poor gross and/or fine motor skills

- moves around clumsily.

They may have visual difficulties if they

- hold books and objects close to their face to look at them

- always sit at the front for stories or television and then strain to look at the book or TV

- bang into or trip over objects

- have a lack of confidence when moving around the room and/or show anxiety about banging into things

- find difficulty in focusing on an object or have problems in eye tracking

- have difficulty in doing activities that require visual skills and/or have difficulty with hand–eye coordination

- have unusual eye movements such as roving or 'trembling' of the eyeball

- display abnormal social interaction or autistic-type behaviours

- hold their head in an unusual position

- display eye poking, rocking or other 'blindisms'.

They may have hearing difficulties if they

- concentrate intensively on the faces and body gestures of the adults in the setting

- either don't follow instructions, follow instructions only sometimes, and/or follow instructions wrongly

- don't respond to their name, especially if you call them from behind

- watch the other children before doing an action, and then copy the others

- appear to need more visual input and support during activities than the other children in the group

- behave inappropriately or seem to be frustrated without any apparent cause

- don't react to loud or unexpected noises

- shout or talk too loudly without realising it

- have delayed speech or speech that's difficult to understand

- change their voice tone while they're speaking

- have difficulty doing activities that require listening skills

- have discharges from their ear(s), which don't seem to clear up or which occur quite frequently

- tilt their head when listening to stories, instructions and so on

- appear to be in a world of their own or showing autistic-type behaviours.

Expression of Concern Form

Name of setting: Dales View Nursery   **Child's name:** Kieran Smith

Date of Birth: 18.04.00   **Date of admission:** 13.03.04

Area of concern: Lack of social interaction with adults & children

Area(s) of learning affected [tick boxes as appropriate]:

Personal, social and emotional development ✔   Physical development ☐

Communication, language and literacy ✔   Creative development ☐

Mathematical development ☐   Knowledge and understanding of the world ☐

Date(s) of observation(s): 14/16/19 Apr. 04   **Type of observation:** Focused (15 mins)

Findings of observation(s):

Kieran's lack of interaction occurred mainly in the work areas (especially when he was in smaller groups) and the playground. He usually refused to join in singing or action rhymes, or to answer other children's questions/invitations to play. He seemed to be reluctant to use the toys or books except when he was alone. His play was usually solitary.

Date(s) of assessment(s): None yet done   **Assessment(s) used:**

Findings of assessment(s):

Action taken: Key worker allocated to Kieran to support him during group sessions and help him achieve specific Stepping Stones from the Foundation Stage curriculum (see Kieran's Small steps planning form).

Have the parents been consulted? Yes/~~No~~   **Parent's signature:** *Annie Smith*

Has the SENCO been consulted? Yes/~~No~~ (told but not yet involved)

Signed: Clare Hampton   **Position:** Nursery Nurse

Date: 20 April 2004   **Date review due:** 20.07.04

ACTIVITY

Complete the Expression of Concern Form with a partner. If possible use a real child and fill in each section following discussion together.

Expression of Concern Form

Name of setting: _____   Child's name: _____

Date of Birth: _____   Date of admission: _____

Area of concern: _____

Area(s) of learning affected [tick boxes as appropriate]:

Personal, social and emotional development ☐   Physical development ☐

Communication, language and literacy ☐   Creative development ☐

Mathematical development ☐   Knowledge and understanding of the world ☐

Date(s) of observation(s): _____   Type of observation: _____

Findings of observation(s):

Date(s) of assessment(s): _____   Assessment(s) used: _____

Findings of assessment(s):

Action taken:

Have the parents been consulted? Yes/No   Parent's signature: _____

Has the SENCO been consulted? Yes/No

Signed: _____   Position: _____

Date: _____   Date review due: _____

Individual Education Plans (IEPs) are decided on and planned by the

- practitioner
- child's parents
- SENCO
- child, if possible.

There isn't a short cut to planning IEPs – they're unique and specific to the child. There's a good reason why they're called *Individual* Education Plans!

The targets of IEPs should be **SMART:**

- **S**pecific – written concisely so everybody knows exactly **what** the child's aims are
- **M**easurable – so everybody knows exactly **when** the aims have been achieved
- **A**chievable – so everybody knows the targets **can** be reached and **how** the child will do this
- **R**ecorded – so everybody knows the **progress** being made
- **T**ime-defined – so everybody knows **by when** (i.e. the date) the targets should be achieved.

- The Individual Education Plan (IEP) should target the child's difficulties **from the point of their strengths**.

- Don't overload the child when you choose their targets. Choose only as many as the child can manage.

- Choose the targets according to the child's needs and achievement level.

- Where possible, link them in with the relevant curriculum goals or targets.

- Always select the targets from the point that the child has already reached and has experienced success with.

- Write the targets concisely, avoiding jargon.

- Specify how you'll know when the child has achieved the target. Make the criteria achievable to avoid failure. You can always make the criteria tougher if the child achieves them too easily.

- Decide the 'rewards' to acknowledge and celebrate success. Let the child choose – rewards must be meaningful for them. To avoid creating a distinction between 'work' and 'play', never use a 'play' session as a reward.

3. Writing effective Individual Education Plans

- Record when the child's performance was checked, by whom and with what result. These details are very important and may be crucial at a later stage.

- Celebrate the child's strengths. This is vital to avoid getting bogged down in what they can't do. There'll be lots of things that they *can* do, and do well, so acknowledge these.

- Check the targets already achieved – they may need to be taught again or revised. Never move the child on until they've consolidated the earlier skills.

- If an Individual Education Plan (IEP) is failing the child, try again with new ideas. This is part of professionalism: have the integrity to acknowledge that a plan isn't working, and change it.

Individual Education Plan

Child's name: Harry Jones   **DOB:** 29.03.00

Date IEP implemented: 13.01.04   **Code of Practice level:** E Y Action

Areas of strength: Harry enjoys books; he paints excellent pictures.

Areas of difficulty: Harry has difficulty with early number work. He has hearing problems – he's got grommets; he regularly attends the ear nose & throat department at the hospital.

Targets to be reached by: 8.04.03

1) Harry will be able to count from 1 to 4 using apparatus.

2) Harry will be able to recognise and name 1 to 4 when shown in written form.

3) Harry will be able to write any numeral from 1 to 4 on request.

Criteria for success:

1) Harry will count from 1 to 4 using four different types of apparatus, 4 times out of 5.

2) Harry will recognise and name 1, 2 , 3 or 4 in written form in a variety of places, 4 times out of 5.

3) Harry will correctly write a requested numeral from 1 to 4, 4 times out of 5.

Teaching methods: initially in a one-to-one situation in the quiet area; then in the main nursery areas to use counting displays, posters, name tags, etc.

Staff involved: Mrs Smith, early years teacher; Mrs Scott, nursery nurse; Mrs Jones, mother, to work at home.

Frequency of programme: twice daily (morning and afternoon) for a maximum of ten minutes, five days per week; once per evening at home when possible.

Equipment/Apparatus: cubes, counters, plastic sorting shapes, any appropriate counting apparatus of Harry's choice, paper, pencils and felt-tip pens.

Date of next review: 9.04.04

To be attended by Mrs Smith, Mrs Scott & Mrs Jones.

ACTIVITY

Complete the Individual Education Plan (IEP) Form with a partner. If possible, use a real child and fill in each section following discussion together.

Individual Education Plan

Child's name: DOB:

Date IEP implemented: Code of Practice level:

Areas of strength:

Areas of difficulty:

Targets to be reached by:

1)

2)

3)

Criteria for success:

1)

2)

3)

Teaching methods:

Staff involved:

Frequency of programme:

Equipment/Apparatus:

Date of next review:

Record of Staff SEN Training

Name	Date of training	Course attended	Purpose of course	Provider	Value (scale 1–10)

Chapter 4

Supporting the children – making sure their entitlements are met

---

The **key points** covered in this chapter are:

- Identifying a difficulty and expressing concern.

- The three phases of the *Special Educational Needs (SEN) Code of Practice* (Early Years Action, Early Years Action Plus, Statutory Assessment) and the SENCO's role in each phase.

- The practicalities of planning, writing and using Individual Education Plans (IEPs).

- Organising and holding reviews – some suggestions and ideas.

INTRODUCTION

Here we'll be exploring the issues around the core of this book: the child. 'Catching 'em young' and supporting them fully are their entitlements. As practitioners responsible for helping the little ones in our care to achieve their potential, we must strive to become experts and use that expertise professionally.

As professionals, we are here for the child – the child is not here for us.

IDENTIFYING A DIFFICULTY

If the child's key worker has a concern about a child, they should:

- ask the child's parents for permission to speak to you as SENCO;

- observe and assess the child, recording the results objectively;

- complete a form expressing their concerns, involving the parents in this;

- differentiate the child's curriculum;

- monitor and record the child's progress closely, informing both the parents and you of outcomes;

- review, together with the parents and you, whether and when the child needs to move to Early Years Action.

Observations highlight what the child can do, and should be done in a variety of situations – for example, self-chosen activities, structured activities, adult-led activities and play activities – so building up a picture of the child's achievements and abilities. Use the information to assess the child's general achievement level, and to plan their next targets. Share the information with everybody involved, helping them gain a fuller insight into the child's abilities. You'll find a more detailed discussion of observations in Chapter 5.

EXPRESSING CONCERN

Make sure the child's parents are happy with what you've written on the Expression of Concern Form. Some parents may feel anxious or threatened so try not to make it stressful for them. Avoid words like 'register' or 'official', which may have negative associations. This might be the beginning of a long-term partnership between you and the parents, and it's important from the outset that they trust you and have confidence in you.

Figure 4.1 shows an example of a completed Expression of Concern Form.

There's a blank photocopiable version of the form on page 82 to use as it stands or adapt to suit your own needs.

Differentiated Learning Plans

The child's curriculum should be differentiated to support their learning. Adapt the activities, presentation, teaching styles, timing and so on, enabling the child to achieve the target skill or concept. Break down the final target into small steps, done one at a time and thoroughly consolidated before moving on to the next one. Thus the child learns through a graduated approach, allowing for their personal learning style and level. Record the plan on a form such as the example of a completed Differentiated Learning Plan Form shown in Figure 4.2.

There's a blank photocopiable version of the form on page 83 to use as it stands or adapt to suit your own situation.

Figure 4.1   An example of a completed Expression of Concern Form

Expression of Concern Form

Name of setting: Dales View Nursery   **Child's name:** Kieran Smith

Date of Birth: 18.04.00   **Date of admission:** 13.03.04

Area of concern: Lack of social interaction with adults & children

Area(s) of learning affected [tick boxes as appropriate]:

Personal, social and emotional development ☑   Physical development ☐

Communication, language and literacy ☑   Creative development ☐

Mathematical development ☐   Knowledge and understanding of the world ☐

Date(s) of observation(s): 14/16/19 Apr. 04   **Type of observation:** Focused (15 mins)

Findings of observation(s):

Kieran's lack of interaction occurred mainly in the work areas (especially when he was in smaller groups) and the playground. He usually refused to join in singing or action rhymes, or to answer other children's questions/invitations to play. He seemed to be reluctant to use the toys or books except when he was alone. His play was usually solitary.

Date(s) of assessment(s): None yet done   **Assessment(s) used:**

Findings of assessment(s):

Action taken: Key worker allocated to Kieran to support him during group sessions and help him achieve specific Stepping Stones from the Foundation Stage curriculum (see Kieran's Small steps planning form).

Have the parents been consulted? Yes/~~No~~   **Parent's signature:** *Annie Smith*

Has the SENCO been consulted? Yes/~~No~~ (told but not yet involved)

Signed: Clare Hampton   **Position:** Nursery Nurse

Date: 20.04.04   **Date review due:** 20.07.04

Figure 4.2 An example of a completed Differentiated Learning Plan

Differentiated Learning Plan

Child's name: Mary Ann Jones   **Area of concern:** Self-help skills

Area of Learning: Personal, social and emotional development

~~Stepping Stone~~/Early Learning Goal [delete as appropriate]:

Dress and undress independently and manage their own personal hygiene

Small steps to target:	Date achieved	Date checked
1. Mary Ann will put on her coat with help from a supporter before each playtime. She will fasten the final button after the supporter has put her arms into the sleeves & shown her how to fasten the other buttons.	13.02.04	17.02.04
2. Mary Ann will fasten the last button when dressing up in the Home Corner, after the helper has put her arms in the sleeves & done the other buttons.	17.02.04	20.02.04
3. Mary Ann will fasten the last two buttons of her coat each time she puts it on, after a helper has put her arms in the sleeves & done the other buttons.	20.02.04	24.02.04
4. Mary Ann will fasten half of her coat buttons after the helper has put her arms in the sleeves & done the other buttons.	27.02.04	
5. Mary Ann will fasten all her buttons independently when dressing.		
6. Mary Ann will put her arms into her coat before going out.		

Equipment and materials: Button-matching game; Mary Ann's clothes; button-fastening game; dressing up clothes

Staff involved: Clare Hampton and Maria Davies (daily sessions)

Home support/follow-up: We have asked Mary Ann's Mum to put Mary Ann's buttoned coat on rather than her zipped one. We'll also practise with the buttons in her other garments (cardigans , blouses, etc.). Mary Ann takes home the button-matching game to play with over the weekends.

EARLY YEARS ACTION

If you're still worried about the child, despite their differentiated curriculum, then move to Early Years Action, by planning, writing and implementing an IEP for the child, practitioner and parents to work from. (You can also involve the parents by designing a Play Plan together. This is a framework for the parents to follow up at home the work you're doing in the setting. Its targets are linked with those of the IEP, and the supporting activities are always play oriented, with games and fun things to do. There's a fuller discussion of Play Plans in Chapter 6.)

Remember – **it is not your role to implement every child's IEP,** unless you're the child's key worker. There's a common misperception that it's the SENCO's job to teach the child or work with them on the IEP, regardless of who is the child's primary practitioner. Try to resist any pressure for you to take this on – you have enough to do implementing the IEPs of 'your' children, as well as fulfilling your other roles as SENCO.

If you *are* experiencing this type of difficulty, ask your manager or head to support you by explaining your role and position to the other practitioners in the setting. Show them the relevant parts of the *SEN Code of Practice* to highlight your point – Section 4:16. (Make sure, however, that your colleagues are receiving the support and help *they* need. It's possible they're pressurising you to 'do' the IEPs because they're feeling insecure, threatened or deskilled, and would appreciate some help themselves.)

IEPs are decided by the practitioner, the child's parents, you as SENCO (although if you're not the key worker, your input will be limited) and, if possible, the child, at a level that's appropriate for them. Their age isn't important since even very young children can be involved. For example, they could choose from selected equipment or decide from several options of activity. There isn't a short cut to planning IEPs which are unique and specific to the child – there's a good reason why they're called *Individual* Education Plans!

The IEP should target the child's difficulties **from the point of their strengths.** Don't overload the child when you choose their targets – the *SEN Code* says a *maximum* of three or four targets, so you can choose only as many as the child can manage. If this means only one or two, then that's fine – just note it on the IEP. Choose the targets according to the child's needs and achievement level, and where possible, link them in with the relevant curriculum goals or targets. Always select the targets from the point that the child has already reached and has experienced success with.

Here are a few handy hints for planning IEPs:

- Write the targets concisely, avoiding jargon.

- Specify how you'll know when the child has achieved the target. Make the criteria achievable to avoid failure. You can always make the criteria tougher if the child achieves them too easily.

- Decide the 'rewards' to acknowledge and celebrate success. Let the child choose – rewards must be meaningful for them. To avoid creating a distinction between 'work' and 'play', never use a 'play' session as a reward.

- Record when the child's performance was checked, by whom and with what result. These details are very important and may be crucial at a later stage.

- Celebrate the child's strengths. This is vital to avoid getting bogged down in what they can't do. There'll be lots of things that they *can* do, and do well, so acknowledge these.

- Check the targets already achieved – they may need to be taught again or revised. Never move the child on until they've consolidated the earlier skills.

- If an IEP is failing the child, try again with new ideas. This is part of professionalism: have the integrity to acknowledge that a plan isn't working, and change it.

Figure 4.3 shows an example of a completed IEP Form.

There's a blank photocopiable version of the form on page 84 to use as it stands or adapt to suit your own requirements.

In the meantime, you as SENCO have other responsibilities.

- Tell the child's parents about the Local Education Authority (LEA)'s Parent Partnership Service (PPS) and give them all the LEA's available information. For non-English speakers, contact the translation services offered by the LEA's PPS.

- Collect all the setting's information about the child. Don't involve volunteers who come into the setting, particularly if they're non-professionals. Their input can only be anecdotal and won't have any legal standing. Above all, the child's rights to confidentiality must be respected and protected, and volunteers must not have access to private information regarding the child's difficulties.

- Collect any relevant information from outside agents who may be involved, such as a social worker or the health visitor.

- If appropriate, liaise with the educational psychologist (EP). This may be only on a 'need to know' basis and must be done *with the parents' permission*. If they're anxious about it, be sure to handle the situation with great sensitivity.

- Arrange a review meeting at least once every three months. You may need to do this more often, every six weeks or so, depending on the situation and the child's age.

Figure 4.3 An example of a completed Individual Education Plan

Individual Education Plan

Child's name: Harry Jones   **DOB:** 29.03.00

Date IEP implemented: 13.01.04   **Code of Practice level:** E Y Action

Areas of strength: Harry enjoys books; he paints excellent pictures.

Areas of difficulty: Harry has difficulty with early number work. He has hearing problems – he's got grommets; he regularly attends the ear nose & throat department at the hospital.

Targets to be reached by: 8.04.03

1) Harry will be able to count from 1 to 4 using apparatus.

2) Harry will be able to recognise and name 1 to 4 when shown in written form.

3) Harry will be able to write any numeral from 1 to 4 on request.

Criteria for success:

1) Harry will count from 1 to 4 using four different types of apparatus, 4 times out of 5.

2) Harry will recognise and name 1, 2 , 3 or 4 in written form in a variety of places, 4 times out of 5.

3) Harry will correctly write a requested numeral from 1 to 4, 4 times out of 5.

Teaching methods: initially in a one-to-one situation in the quiet area; then in the main nursery areas to use counting displays, posters, name tags, etc.

Staff involved: Mrs Smith, early years teacher; Mrs Scott, nursery nurse; Mrs Jones, mother, to work at home.

Frequency of programme: twice daily (morning and afternoon) for a maximum of ten minutes, five days per week; once per evening at home when possible.

Equipment/Apparatus: cubes, counters, plastic sorting shapes, any appropriate counting apparatus of Harry's choice, paper, pencils and felt-tip pens.

Date of next review: 9.04.04

To be attended by Mrs Smith, Mrs Scott & Mrs Jones.

IEP reviews

Forward planning, organisation and a shared but confidential calendar or diary in the setting result in successful reviews. As SENCO, you're responsible for organising the reviews that are held at the earlier levels of SEN provision. (The LEA usually coordinates the Annual Review of Statements.) Here are some practical suggestions for planning a review.

- Put trigger-reminders in the diary, working backwards from the review date. Plan about four weeks before the review date and jot down a note on each appropriate date, for the things you need to do. For example:

12.03.04 (i.e. four weeks ahead) Walter Smith's review due on 9.04.04. Request information and advice from:

Walter's parents and Walter

Mrs Dodd (early years teacher)

Mrs Jones (nursery nurse)

Mr Muir (educational psychologist)

Advice to be received by 26.03.04.

22.03.04 (i.e. two and a half weeks ahead) Advice received so far from Mrs Dodd, Mrs James.

Remind Mr & Mrs Smith and Mr Muir that advice is due by 26.03.04.

26.03.04 (i.e. two weeks ahead) Send out invitations & advice documents for Walter Smith's review.

7.04.04 (i.e. the day before) Get coffee, biscuits and flowers for Walter Smith's review.

8.04.04 Walter Smith's review: 10.00 a.m.

- If English isn't the parents' first language, arrange for an interpreter.

- On review day, make the room cheerful and welcoming, with coffee and biscuits and some flowers. Help the parents to relax by inviting them a few minutes earlier.

- Arrange chairs in a circle, with a low table in the middle. Some parents feel threatened or intimidated by the review, so don't organise the room as if for a formal interview.

- Work your way through the Review Form systematically, helping to keep everybody focused on each point as it comes up for discussion.

- Ask for the key worker's contribution, which is crucial, as they know the child most intimately within the setting.

- Invite the other agents' contributions, if relevant.

- Ensure that the parents and the child, if appropriate, can offer their input. You can design a Parent's Review Form to give to the parents some time before the review and which helps them to focus on what to say in the meeting. Figure 4.4 shows an example of a completed Parent's Review Form, and you'll find a blank photocopiable version of the form on page 85.

If the child isn't there but is able to make a contribution to the discussion, they can do this through the parents on a Child's Review Form. Encourage them to record on it what the child says or thinks about the IEP, their progress and so on. Talk the form through with the parents and make sure they are happy about completing it. Figure 4.5 shows an example of a completed Child's Review Form.

There's a blank photocopiable Child's Review Form on page 86.

During the review:

- Make sure that everybody has time to speak but don't let people hog the limelight. As Chair, you can bring the focus back to the discussion and give the other people present a chance to have their say.

- Include a plan of further action. On the Review Form, you can record this as a simple *Yes/No* deletion.

- Conclude by briefly summarising what was said, asking whether everybody agrees. Clear up any misunderstandings immediately and ask everybody to initial your notes before they leave.

- Book the date of the next review immediately.

- Sign and date the Review Form. If possible, give the parents a copy immediately.

- Have a quiet word with the parents to make sure they're happy with the review's outcome. This is especially important for parents who are shy, or who feel upset or threatened by the process. They may need to have some of the paperwork explained to them, especially if they have language and/or literacy difficulties themselves. Make sure you do this sensitively and in a supportive way.

- Circulate copies of the Review Form to everybody who attended the meeting as soon as possible so that any queries can be clarified more or less straight away. Also send a copy to the relevant people who didn't attend.

Figure 4.4 An example of a completed Parent's Review Form

Parent's Review Form

Name of child: *Sadie Hampton*   Date of child's birth: *9.01.00*

Your child's health:

Is your child usually healthy? *Yes apart from her asthma*

Do they take any medicines? If so, what are they? *Inhaler mostly in winter*

Have these changed within the last two months? *No*

Your child at home:

Does your child have any hobbies? *She goes to brownies*

What does your child enjoy doing at home? *Playing with her dolls & helping me bake*

What does your child need help with at home? *Her reading and number*

Your child in Catton Lea Nursery School

Is your child happy to come to our setting? *Usually*

Are you happy about the way we support your child in the setting? *Yes*

Are you pleased with your child's progress? *Yes*

Do you have any worries about your child's Individual Education Plan (IEP)? If so, what?
I think she needs to do more work on her reading

Is there anything you think we need to change? If so, what?
I think her targets should be easier because she still isn't reading

What's next for your child?

Are you happy with the targets on your child's IEP?
Yes — I think it's important to concentrate on her reading and maths work

What do you think your child should learn next?
More concentration. I think she needs to learn to keep her head down

Do you have any questions to ask at the review?
Who are you going to contact about Sadie? Will we be able to come to the meetings? Will she have to leave Catton Lea? I don't want her going to a special school

Figure 4.5 **An example of a completed Child's Review Form**

Child's Review Form

My name is *Marco Camilleri*

I was born on *12 September 2000*

I like *playing football. I like making models and dressing up in the home corner.*

. . . .

. . . .

. . . .

I worry about *reading and the computer. Sometimes Mrs Scott shouts at me*

. . . .

. . . .

. . . .

I still need help with *reading my books and learning the sounds.* . . . .

. . . .

. . . .

For my next IEP, I want to *do more games like I play with Mrs Scott*
to help me with my letter matching. I like the bingo on the computer. . . . .

. . . .

Parent's signature *Antonio Camilleri*

Date *19 May 2004*

Figure 4.6 provides an example of a completed Review Form.

You will find a blank photocopiable version of the form on page 87.

You must monitor the child between reviews in case the IEP isn't working. If you think you've done some poor planning, it's crucial that you act immediately. Call an interim review to discuss your concerns with parents and other staff involved, and then change the IEP.

EARLY YEARS ACTION PLUS

This is the stage when you ask for the advice of an outside specialist. You usually refer to outside agents because your setting isn't able to offer the expertise needed to manage the child's difficulties. The multi-agency approach widens here, with everybody benefiting from a broader spectrum of information. Everyone should cooperate closely, with regular liaison, to ensure seamless and better quality provision. The *SEN Code of Practice* gives useful general guidelines about why and when you should refer a child to an outside agent (Section 4:31).

Outside agents

External professionals include the following:

- *The LEA's support services for learning difficulties, speech and language difficulties, visual and hearing impairment and physical disabilities.* These can provide advice on teaching techniques and strategies, setting management, curriculum materials, curriculum development, direct teaching or practical support for practitioners, part-time specialist help, or access to learning support assistance. You should have contact details for these services. If not, the SEN section of your LEA will be able to supply them, or your Area SENCO will be able to advise you. If your setting is private or non-maintained, link up with your local state-maintained early years providers to share information, facilities, services and best practice.

- *The child or educational psychology services,* which carry out more specialised assessments, suggest problem-solving strategies (including techniques in managing behaviour) and evaluate individual children's progress. They can also offer information and advice about the development of your SEN policy and assist with professional development in the area of SEN, as well as helping to promote inclusion.

- *The behaviour support service.*

- *Advisers or teachers of information and communications technology (ICT) for children with additional needs.*

- *Social services.*

Figure 4.6 **An example of a completed IEP Review Form**

IEP Review Form

Child's name: John Davies   **DOB:** 31.01.00

Level: Early Years Action/~~Early Years Action Plus~~ [delete as appropriate]

Date of review: 9.04.04   ~~1st~~/2nd/3rd review [delete as appropriate]

Present at review: Mr & Mrs Davies (parents) Mrs Simpson (teacher)
Mrs Frampton (SENCO)

Report of child's progress/IEP:

1) John can count three items of a variety of apparatus correctly; he still needs to count from 1.

2) John can recognise and name 1 & 2 when shown in written form in a variety of places.

3) John can write 1 & 2 when asked.

The targets have still to be achieved and the criteria need to be reduced. John continues to have difficulties both at home and in the setting.

Additional comments/reports from people not present:

a) Mrs Davies read out John's opinion (see attached Child's Review Form).

John has been happier since the IEP was put in place and he enjoys doing his activities. He says it is hard though and he thinks that his targets are too difficult because he can't remember his work from the day before.

b) Mrs O'Halloran (nursery nurse) reports that John concentrates well but has difficulty in retaining the concept for longer than a few minutes (see attached detailed report).

c)

Further action:

Adjust targets to learn numbers 1–3. SENCO to request input from Early Years Learning Support Service.

Continue with IEP?	Yes/~~No~~
Modify IEP?	Yes/~~No~~
Remain at present stage?	~~Yes~~/No
Move to next stage?	Yes/~~No~~
Discontinue SEN procedure?	~~Yes~~/No
Other action?	Yes/~~No~~ (See 'Further action' above)

Next review due: 21.05.04 (6 weeks)

Name: A. FRAMPTON (SENCO)   **Signed:** A. Frampton
Date: 9.04.04

© Collette Drifte, *A Manual for the Early Years SENCO*, Paul Chapman Publishing, 2005

● *Child protection services.*

● *Medical services,* including health visitors (HVs), paediatric nurses and/or paediatricians, nurses, community or hospital-based paediatricians, child psychiatrists, general practitioners (GPs), physiotherapists, speech and language therapists, occupational therapists and hospital-based counsellors. If the child comes with an identified problem, any combination of these professionals is likely to be already involved. If you identify a difficulty, after consulting with the child's parents, you'll probably liaise initially with the local HV or the child's GP.

● *Private and voluntary organisations,* which are a valuable source of help and information.

You must establish positive and cooperative relations with these agencies. They're very important for the early identification of difficulties and in advising you on effective strategies aimed at preventing further problems developing. As well as these mutual benefits of shared expertise, the liaison and cooperative approach will become a normal part of your policy on special educational needs long before you need to call the agents in. The multi-agency approach should be child centred and flexible, making sure that support for the child continues to be appropriate, even when their needs change.

● BUYER BEWARE!

● If you decide to commission freelance or private specialists or organisations, there are several serious considerations to keep in mind. You (or your setting's manager or head) must check the qualifications and experience of the agents you buy in. You must make sure that all police checks and clearances have been done, and also be aware that your setting, rather than the LEA, will usually have to pay for these outside agents or services.

● If parents share with you reports, assessments or other information about the child that they themselves have commissioned from private providers, make sure you check the credentials of the provider before you rely on their documentation.

● Making a referral

As SENCO, you'll make the referral. However, you, the practitioner, the child's parents and, where possible, the child will have decided that this is the plan of action. After you've asked for outside help, you'll be responsible for *coordinating* the SEN provision made for the child and for any decisions made about this. (NB: *coordinating* the provision – not necessarily *providing* or *implementing* it, unless you're the key worker or named practitioner.)

Your LEA should have a set procedure for maintained settings to make referrals to outside agents. Private and voluntary settings should link up with their local early years establishments to find out about the procedure and to take advantage of the advice and support on offer. There are several things you should do before actually sending off a referral to an outside specialist.

- Hold a review with the child's parents and, if possible, the child. Discuss the IEPs and the child's progress (or lack of it), ask for the parents' and the child's views and decide if you need more information for the referral. Record on the Review Form that you're going to make a referral and to whom.

- Everybody should agree what's to go on the Referral Form. Use blank copies of the form at the review meeting to draft the main points of the referral. As SENCO, you'll be completing the form, so it's important that you have all the necessary information and everybody's agreement before the meeting finishes.

- Collect all the relevant information that the outside agent will need (e.g. the IEPs, the review forms, records of observations, assessments or profiles, samples of the child's work that illustrate their difficulties) to give an overview of the child and their problems. Don't involve volunteers or helpers in this information-gathering process.

- Complete the Referral Form and, together with all the appropriate records and information, send it to the outside agent involved.

Figure 4.7 shows an example of a completed Referral Form.

You'll find a blank photocopiable version of the form on page 88.

The outside agent will meet with the key practitioner, yourself, the parents and the child, if possible. They may also want to make a preliminary assessment of the child. This will be more specialised than any you've done, and will focus more specifically on the child's difficulties.

At the initial meeting you'll have a chance to draw on the advice and suggestions made by the specialist and to plan a new IEP together with them. This should incorporate some of the strategies and suggestions made by the specialist. It's crucial that the parents and the child have the chance to contribute to the planning of the IEP. They won't have the agent's specialised knowledge, but they do have their own expertise to offer. For example, they'll be able to say whether a proposed method of incentive-and-reward will work, whether a target is attractive and whether the activities are exciting – all important considerations if the new IEP is to work.

The implementation of the new IEP is done by the child, the parents and the key practitioner, with you overseeing its implementation. Usually the outside specialist monitors the programme and offers ongoing advice. How often they visit will depend on things such as their workload, the seriousness of the child's difficulties and the amount of support you need.

Figure 4.7 **An example of a completed Referral Form**

Child's name: Sarah James   DOB: 18.04.00

Date of referral: 14.08.04   Name of setting: Catton Lea Nursery

Name of main practitioner: Polly Carlton

Name of SENCO: Maria Dwyer

Area(s) of concern [tick boxes as appropriate]:

Personal, social and emotional   Physical development ☐
development ☑

Communication, language and literacy ☐   Creative development ☐

Mathematical development ☐   Knowledge and understanding of the
                                             world ☐

Have IEPs been put in place? Yes/~~No~~   Are copies of IEPs enclosed? Yes/~~No~~

If not, please state reason . . . .
. . . .

If other records/documents are enclosed, please state what: Examples of Sarah's paintings;
Foundation Stage profile

Has the SENCO been involved? Yes/~~No~~

If not, please state reason:. . . . .
. . . .

Have the parents/carers been involved? ~~Yes~~/No

If not, please state reason: Sarah's parents did not want to be involved with doing the IEPs at home.

Has the child been involved? Yes/~~No~~.

If not, please state reason: . . . .
. . . .

Reason(s) for referral (this should be signed by each practitioner who makes a contribution):

Sarah's concentration span is no more than one or two minutes – she finds difficulty in staying
on task with any single activity for longer than 35 seconds. Her maximum time is when she is
doing a jigsaw. Her play is usually solitary and she finds it difficult to be in group situations
without becoming aggressive towards one of the other children. IEPs targeting these difficulties
haven't helped Sarah develop positive behaviour and we need more specialised advice and support.
We are concerned that her paintings and drawings are almost always about crying children.

Polly Carlton, Nursery Nurse

Signature of referring practitioner: Maria Dwyer

Position: SENCO

Signature of parent/carer: Ann James

Your other responsibilities as SENCO continue in the meantime.

- Make sure the child's parents are still completely involved and informed about their child's progress. (You must tell them of any unscheduled visits made by the outside specialist and what was discussed.)

- Relay any advice and support from external agent to both the child's key worker and their parents.

- Liaise with the specialist agent(s), the child's key worker and their parents to monitor the new IEP, the targets, and the teaching strategies. You'll then be able to act swiftly if the IEP is failing to support the child.

- Ensure that the IEP is reviewed at least every three months/once per term, remembering that you can call an interim meeting if there's a serious concern to discuss.

- Ensure the records of the new IEPs are kept up to date and carefully maintained. If the child is eventually referred for a Statutory Assessment, the LEA will ask you for evidence of the differentiated work done with the child. The IEPs will form the main body of this strand of the evidence.

STATUTORY ASSESSMENT

Between 1 and 2 per cent of children will continue to cause concern and those involved may decide to refer the child to the LEA for a Statutory Assessment. The three main sources of referral are: early years settings, the child's parents, or other agencies.

Early years settings

If your setting is maintained or in receipt of government funding, you have a statutory right to refer a child for assessment if the child is three years or older. Childminders or private nurseries can bring a child to the attention of the LEA, which then decides whether a Statutory Assessment is required.

Parents

Parents may decide to refer their child for a Statutory Assessment. The LEA then must carry out the request

- unless a Statutory Assessment has already been done on the child in the six months before the referral; or

- unless the LEA feels the assessment is unnecessary having considered all the evidence supplied in support of the referral.

The LEA must inform you if the parents have made a referral and they must decide within six weeks of a referral whether they will carry out the assessment. Where you and the parents have been working together, you've probably agreed to the parental referral. Sometimes, however, the parents may be unhappy about the way the setting has dealt with their child's difficulties and they decide to make the referral independently. When this happens, the LEA must consider the referral and take appropriate action.

Other agencies

This is usually done by a professional from health or social services, and usually concerns a child under five who has complex or profound difficulties. The LEA will collect evidence in the same way as they do for referrals through education professionals.

How is a referral made?

There's a standard procedure to follow, normally entailing you working with the educational psychologist (EP) who will advise you on completing the forms and gathering together the required documentation. The referral itself is usually made on the LEA's official form. You must include:

- the parents' views, as recorded on earlier review forms (they may also like to send an additional statement);
- the child's views from the review records, but also through involvement of the child in the actual referral process;
- copies of all the IEPs;
- evidence of the child's progress (e.g. records of achievement, profiles, etc.);
- other relevant records, information or advice on health-related matters from the HV, the child's GP or the speech and language therapist;
- the reports by and evidence of the involvement of outside agents;
- evidence to show to what extent you actually followed the advice of the outside agents.

Statutory Assessment procedure

Next, you send the whole package to the LEA, which must decide within six weeks whether to go ahead with a Statutory Assessment of the child. The LEA is obliged to write to the parents outlining the procedures involved in deciding on an assessment, informing them of their rights, advising them about the PPS and asking whether they would like the LEA to consult any other professionals if an assessment goes ahead.

Within this six-week period, the child's parents have 29 days to inform the LEA whether they agree or not with the referral going ahead. If they agree, they don't have to wait for the 29 days to expire, but they can tell the LEA at the beginning, so the LEA can start the process immediately.

Sometimes the LEA turns down a request for a Statutory Assessment and if so, it must write to the child's parents and you, giving the reasons why. The parents have the right to appeal to the SEN Tribunal if they disagree with the LEA's decision.

Once the LEA decide to make a Statutory Assessment they have to follow a strict timetable. There's a useful flow chart of this in the *SEN Code of Practice* on page 120. (Spot the spelling mistake at the point where the LEA decides whether to assess the child!) The LEA must complete the process within the following ten weeks, because they then must decide whether to start the next stage, which is the issuing of a Statement of Special Educational Needs.

At the start of the assessment process, the LEA will contact the child's parents, all the professionals involved with the child, and the EP for their opinions and advice regarding the child's current progress.

You and the key worker will have an overview of the child's achievements in relation to their peer group and the Foundation Stage curriculum. You'll know which strategies were successful and which were less effective, how the child performed, what they found difficult and what they achieved. You'll also know what the child's learning styles are, how they react to certain activities or situations in the setting, and how they interact with the other children.

Completing the educational advice

The LEA will send you forms for the educational advice. If you're doing this for the first time, don't worry – you'll have all the information you need in the child's records. To help focus thoughts, and to bring together some of the information, think about the following questions:

Communication and language skills

Does the child:

- communicate by speech, gestures, oral sounds or not at all?

- make eye contact during conversations?

- speak clearly?

- always communicate or just sometimes?

- communicate with adults, or the other children, or both, or neither?

- understand what is said to them?

- talk about everything, or just a few topics, or only one?

- use the kind of language expected from a child of that age?

- play imaginatively?

- speak English as their main language? If not, what language is spoken at home?

Social, emotional and personal skills

Does the child:

- interact well with the other children?

- have difficulties with relationships with the adults in the setting?

- share and take turns appropriately?

- get easily upset over small things?

- play happily with other children?

- play happily alone?

- have a reasonable concentration span?

- have any ritualistic or obsessive behaviour (e.g. hand flapping, spinning the wheels on toys, doing the same jigsaw time after time)?

- become distressed at any change in the routine?

- join in group activities and discussions confidently?

- have self-help skills (i.e. are they independent at the toilet, at meals or at dressing)?

Physical skills

Does the child:

- have any physical difficulties?

- have gross motor skills (i.e. can they run, jump, climb, kick a ball, ride a tricycle, hop, skip, etc.)?

- have fine motor skills (i.e. can they manipulate puzzles, do threading or cutting with scissors, use pencils, crayons or paintbrushes, etc.)?

- have good eyesight?

- have good hearing?

Learning abilities

Does the child:

- have difficulties in learning (e.g. with early literacy skills or early mathematical concepts)?

- need lots of repetition and practice before learning a concept?

- seem to learn something one day and forget it the next? Does this happen fairly often?

- predict the next part of a story?

- try to solve problems?

- make simple decisions?

- show curiosity about how things work?

- have an interest in the world around them?

Medical and health issues

Does the child:

- have any known medical condition or disability?

- have any allergies?

- have any special dietary needs?

- need to take medication on a regular basis?

- have any sensory disability (e.g. visual or hearing)?

- have any physical disability?

- have prolonged absences for medical reasons?

A Statutory Assessment of a child doesn't always result in the writing of a Statement of Special Educational Needs since the LEA may decide not to proceed. If so, they must write to both the child's parents and you, explaining why, within two weeks of the completion of the assessment and the making of the decision. They must also outline what provision they think is appropriate to meet the child's needs. Once again, the parents have the right of appeal to the SEN Tribunal if they disagree with the LEA's decision.

However, the LEA may decide to write and issue a Statement of Special Educational Needs, a legally binding document outlining the areas of difficulty being experienced by the child, and the most appropriate provision for meeting their needs. They have to send a draft copy of the Statement to the parents within the same time limit of two weeks, and the final Statement must be written and issued within eight weeks from that point.

In other words, the entire process from initial referral to Statement must not take any longer than 26 weeks.

Once the final Statement has been written, a copy of it must be sent to the child's parents together with details of their right to appeal to the SEN Tribunal, if they disagree with anything in the Statement.

Annual/Biannual Review

A Statement of Special Educational Needs is formally reviewed annually, but if the child is under five, it's reviewed every six months. This is to ensure that the recommendations made in the Statement are still applicable and appropriate. The six-monthly (Biannual) Review isn't as formal or full as the main annual review. The *SEN Code of Practice* enables the Statement to be amended if necessary, at the Biannual Review.

Involving the child

Involving the child in their own planning and decision making helps them to feel confident and happy about the process they've become a part of. Sometimes they'll need help to express their views and opinions, but this doesn't lessen the importance of what they have to say.

- Develop an ethos where individual differences are accepted and respected. Have resources and books that reflect a wide range of abilities and regularly share these with all the children.

- Talk to the child about their difficulties and why they're being assessed, have IEPs and reviews, etc. The key worker is the best person to do this. They must use the vocabulary and style of language that the child's familiar with. For example, if the child knows and uses the term 'adult', then you can refer to the outside agents as 'the adults from a different place who come here to help you', but if the child is more familiar with the term 'grown-up', then use those words.

- Help them to express how they feel about their own difficulties. Talk about their problems and encourage them to say how they feel about it.

- Make sure that the child doesn't focus so much on their difficulties that they think there's nothing else to talk about except their problem. Encourage them to tell you *everything* about themselves, such as their favourite story, film, television programme, toy, game, etc., what makes them laugh or cry, what's their biggest wish, etc. Help them to make a book about themselves, with photos, pictures and what they have said written inside.

- Encourage the child to tell you how they see themselves in the setting. Get them to tell you what they're good at, what they enjoy doing, what they have learned, what they find hard to do, what they don't like doing.

- Help them understand that the things they need help with developing are their additional needs. Use your chosen phrase from the beginning, because the child will hear it a great many times before you've finished the process. Explain that it's the adults' way of describing what things the child needs more help with than other children. You can help them understand by talking in terms of the child's particular difficulties.

- Talk about the outside agents and what their part is in the overall plan. Encourage the child to tell you how they feel about this. Get them to draw or photograph the outside agents for the book about themselves.

- If they go on for Statutory Assessment, help them to understand what the process involves. Again, use the correct terminology; explain that it means everybody will be asked to write what things they are good at, what things they find difficult and what sort of help they need to learn the things they find hard.

- Introduce each member of the team to the child and explain what their job will be. This reassures the child that everybody is working together to make sure the child gets the help they need.

- If a Statement of Special Educational Needs is written, explain to the child that it's just an important paper which has written on it all the things the child needs to help them learn the things they find difficult.

- Prepare the child for any specialised help they may be allocated. Get them to tell you how they feel about this. All of this information will form part of the child's contribution to the Statutory Assessment and/or the Statement.

SUMMARY

The **key points** covered in this chapter were:

- Identifying a difficulty and expressing concern.

- The three phases of the *SEN Code of Practice* and the SENCO's role in each phase.

- The practicalities of planning, writing and using IEPs.

- Organising and holding reviews – some suggestions and ideas.

Expression of Concern Form

Name of setting: _____ Child's name: _____

Date of Birth: _____ Date of admission: _____

Area of concern: _____

Area(s) of learning affected [tick boxes as appropriate]:

Personal, social and emotional development ☐

Physical development ☐

Communication, language and literacy ☐

Creative development ☐

Mathematical development ☐

Knowledge and understanding of the world ☐

Date(s) of observation(s): _____ Type of observation: _____

Findings of observation(s):

Date(s) of assessment(s): _____ Assessment(s) used: _____

Findings of assessment(s):

Action taken:

Have the parents been consulted? Yes/No Parent's signature: _____

Has the SENCO been consulted? Yes/No

Signed: _____ Position: _____

Date: _____ Date review due: _____

Differentiated Learning Plan

Child's name: _____   Area of concern: _____

Area of Learning: _____

Stepping Stone/Early Learning Goal [delete as appropriate]:
_____

Small steps to target:	Date achieved	Date checked
1.		
2.		
3.		
4.		
5.		
6.		

_____

Equipment and materials:

_____

Staff involved:

_____

Home support/follow-up:

Individual Education Plan

Child's name: DOB:

Date IEP implemented: Code of Practice level:

Areas of strength:

Areas of difficulty:

Targets to be reached by:

1)

2)

3)

Criteria for success:

1)

2)

3)

Teaching methods:

Staff involved:

Frequency of programme:

Equipment/Apparatus:

Date of next review:

Parent's Review Form

Name of child: _____   Date of child's birth: _____

Your child's health:

Is your child usually healthy?

Do they take any medicines? If so, what are they?

Have these changed within the last two months?

Your child at home:

Does your child have any hobbies?

What does your child enjoy doing at home?

What does your child need help with at home?

Your child in _____

Is your child happy to come to our setting?

Are you happy about the way we support your child in the setting?

Are you pleased with your child's progress?

Do you have any worries about your child's Individual Education Plan (IEP)? If so, what?

Is there anything you think we need to change? If so, what?

What's next for your child?

Are you happy with the targets on your child's IEP?

What do you think your child should learn next?

Do you have any questions to ask at the review?

Child's Review Form

My name is   _____

I was born on   _____

I like   _____

_____

_____

I worry about   _____

_____

_____

I still need help with   _____

_____

_____

For my next IEP, I want to   _____

_____

_____

Parent's signature _____

Date   _____

IEP Review Form

Child's Name: _____   DOB: _____

Level: Early Years Action/Early Years Action Plus [delete as appropriate]

Date of review: _____   1st/2nd/3rd review [delete as appropriate]

Present at review:

Reports of child's progress / IEP:

Additional comments/reports from people not present:

a)

b)

c)

Further action:

Continue with IEP?	Yes/No
Modify IEP?	Yes/No
Remain at present stage?	Yes/No
Move to next stage?	Yes/No
Discontinue SEN procedure?	Yes/No
Other action?	Yes/No

Next review due: _____

Name: _____   Signed: _____

Date: _____

Referral form to outside agents

Child's name: _____ DOB: _____

Date of referral: _____ Name of setting: _____

Name of main practitioner: _____

Name of SENCO: _____

Area(s) of concern [tick boxes as appropriate]:

Personal, social and emotional development ☐

Physical development ☐

Communication, language and literacy ☐

Creative development ☐

Mathematical development ☐

Knowledge and understanding of the world ☐

Have IEPs been put in place? Yes/No

Are copies of IEPs enclosed? Yes/No

If not, please state reason: _____

_____

If other records/documents are enclosed, please state what: _____

_____

Has the SENCO been involved? Yes/No

If not, please state reason: _____

_____

Have the parents/carers been involved? Yes/No

If not, please state reason: _____

_____

Has the child been involved? Yes/No

If not, please state reason: _____

_____

Reason(s) for referral (this should be signed by each practitioner who makes a contribution):

_____

_____

_____

_____

Signature of referring practitioner: _____

Position: _____

Signature of parent/carer: _____

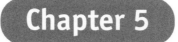

Chapter 5

Keeping track – ensuring effective record keeping

The **key points** covered in this chapter are:

- The crucial importance of setting up and maintaining records.

- The role of the SENCO regarding records.

- The different types of records: observations, assessments, examples of work, profiles and checklists, Individual Education Plans (IEPs), IEP/review summaries.

- Records as evidence.

INTRODUCTION

We live in an age of paper chases and log books, and the special educational needs (SEN) process has records as a fundamental part of its workings. While we moan and groan about filling in forms and pen pushing, the updating and monitoring of the records of the children in our care are crucial. When we put a child on the path set by the *SEN Code of Practice*, we're talking about a long-term objective, with the development of a young human being at its core. It's that child's entitlement to have their progress and achievements, and their areas of continuing need, recorded and acknowledged over the period of time they're being supported.

SETTING UP AND MAINTAINING RECORDS

You can't overemphasise the crucial importance of establishing an effective and accurate system of record keeping for children with additional needs. Only by keeping the first observations and expressions of concern, the ongoing records of progress, and the log of final outcomes can the child's achievements be fully appreciated. It's almost like those 'before' and 'after' photos you see in magazines – good records give an overall picture of how the child has developed and progressed as a result of the support given.

Sometimes a child makes progress in small steps and it's easy to fall into the trap of thinking they're not getting anywhere. Take a look at the first observations, compared with what's happening now, and my guess is you'll see that in fact the child has come on a long way from the early days. It's only through accurate records that this picture is clear.

Sadly, though, some children don't progress very well, for whatever reason. Again, accurate and objective records are vital here to highlight the child's areas of continuing need. If a child has to move through Early Years Action Plus, and even to Statutory Assessment, their records will form the main body of evidence required. We'll discuss this in more detail later in the chapter.

As SENCO, you need to make sure that your setting has a record system whereby the practitioners can collect and log down information about the child who's causing concern. The system should include:

- various methods of gathering information about and evidence of the child's performance;

- a method of expressing concern if their (lack of) progress is worrying;

- a system of recording their differentiated curriculum;

- clear and effective records of programmes of work, or action plans (e.g. Individual Education Plans [IEPs], Play Plans, Individual Programmes of Work, etc. – these are all discussed in greater detail in Chapter 4);

- accurate and practical records of reviews and meetings to monitor the child.

Most settings can access their Local Education Authority (LEA)'s record forms, which keeps the documentation standardised locally. This helps enormously if a child moves from one setting to another, and their records go with them. Private and non-maintained settings could design their own forms if they wished, but, again, it's more practical and sensible to use those from the LEA.

THE ROLE OF THE SENCO REGARDING RECORDS

One of your most important roles as SENCO is to make sure that your colleagues maintain the SEN records. Because many of these already form an integral part of the child's profile, and are working documents, this responsibility shouldn't be onerous. Because, too, the *SEN Code of Practice* directs that IEPs (which are records) are reviewed regularly, they are automatically updated and monitored.

If you can, establish a 'long-term culture' in your setting, whereby everybody is aware that today's records may be needed to form tomorrow's evidence of action. Later in the chapter, we'll explore the importance of this, since the authorities will ask you to demonstrate *through your records* how you supported the child, and whether you did this effectively. This is particularly important when you go on to Early Years Action Plus, with the involvement of outside agents.

You must also emphasise the necessity of honesty and integrity on the part of everybody who writes the child's records. We saw in Chapter 4 that there's no room for pride in this game, for the child's sake. If a Differentiated Learning Plan (DLP), an IEP or Play Plan isn't addressing the child's needs, the practitioners involved must concede this and re-plan. Time lost for these children is lost forever, and they can't afford for that to happen. Writing records, plans or reviews to present a rosy picture of the child's progress, when in fact the little person is struggling with an IEP that's far too challenging, is unethical and unprofessional. The practitioner who records that they got the planning wrong and are trying again has more professional integrity than one who's economical with the truth in order to appear 'successful'. Sadly, some practitioners will do this, and if this is so in your setting, let it be known that you won't tolerate it. The bottom line is that the child pays the price.

You may have to use all your leadership, diplomatic and communication skills, but you must ensure that good practice is developed in your setting. As with many of these things, by setting an example yourself, you'll be demonstrating good practice to your colleagues. Having 'been there and done it' yourself, you'll be in a strong position to encourage colleagues to follow suit.

If somebody appears to be causing concern in this area, check whether they need some support, training, help or advice. They may be feeling overwhelmed by it all, threatened or afraid of the process. Offering to tackle their concerns will go a long way to preventing long-term difficulties, which can only be for the children's benefit.

THE DIFFERENT TYPES OF RECORDS AND HOW THESE ARE USED WHEN PLANNING PROGRAMMES FOR THE CHILD

Let's have a look at the commonest ways we have of recording the children's progress.

Observations

Observations provide a record of what the child can do and you should carry them out in various situations, e.g. play, self-chosen activities, structured activities and adult-led activities. You can then build up an overview of the child's achievements and abilities across the full spectrum of the setting's curriculum.

Observations are also a good way of sharing information about the child with both the parents and other professionals. You can discuss the child with their parents, highlighting your comments from the findings of the observations, so they can see how their child functions in the setting. You can also share the information with other professionals, particularly those who have only just met the child, to help them see the child's full range of abilities.

There are two basic types of observation: the continuous (or narrative) observation and the focused (or targeted) observation.

Continuous (or narrative) observations

Usually all the practitioners in the setting do these. They comprise short notes jotted down at any time on a day-to-day basis, so forming a record of the child's daily progress and any specific achievements, and helping to build up a picture of the child's development in the longer term. They record briefly what the child does, together with short related assessment statements, linking in with the relevant targets of the child's curriculum and/or the IEP. The observer(s) should date and initial the form, and put it into the child's profile folder.

Figure 5.1 shows an example of a completed Continuous Observation Form.

There's a blank photocopiable version of the form on page 106.

Focused (or targeted) observations

Usually only one practitioner in the setting does these, less frequently and with more of a focus. They do the observation across a fixed length of time, usually 10 or 15 minutes, and they record what the child does and says. Normally they'd agree with their colleagues when they'll do the observation, so they can be released from child contact, leading activities or teaching.

All the staff involved with the child should agree how many focused observations should be done per week, per month, half term or term, according to the child's needs. Again, the observer should date and sign the notes.

During the session, the observer can leave out anything the child does that isn't related to the observation focus. So, for example, there isn't any need to write 'Una went to the toilet' if the focus of the observation is to assess Una's early writing skills.

Because of the 'busyness' of early years settings, the observer can make notes with key words and write the observation up properly, either immediately or as soon as possible afterwards.

Figure 5.1   **An example of a completed Continuous Observation Form**

Continuous Observation Form

<u>Child's name:</u> Una Kelly

<u>Date of birth:</u> 22.01.00

<u>Date</u>	<u>Observation</u>	<u>Area of learning</u>	<u>Planning</u>	<u>Observer</u>
14.06.04	Una played with a jigsaw – hard to manipulate the pieces	PSD	More activities for fine motor skills, e.g. thread and beads; straws; jigsaws; etc.	C.M.
14.06.04	Una identified her name on three displays	C L L	Find name in other contexts & identify name card	J.W.
15.06.04	Una destroyed Susan's model	PSD	Plan positive behaviour programme	J.W.

© Collette Drifte, *A Manual for the Early Years SENCO*, Paul Chapman Publishing, 2005

The observation should be objective and factual to ensure accuracy. The record must state only what happened, not the observer's opinion of what happened. For example, 'Una destroyed Susan's model and then hit her' is more objective and factual than 'Una behaved badly towards Susan'. The first statement tells us exactly what Una did; the second shows us that the observer disapproved of what Una did, but nothing else. 'Behaved badly' is a subjective phrase, meaning different things to different people; it doesn't tell the reader anything relevant about the incident.

When you need to collect information about a child who's causing concern, and where specific evidence of that child's difficulties is needed, focused observations are usually better to do than continuous observations. It's very important that you repeat an observation if it seems to illustrate a difficulty that the child is experiencing. One session won't give you enough evidence, so you must observe the child at least once more, preferably a couple more times. Ask another practitioner to do an observation, to discover whether they identify the same concerns, but don't share your feelings beforehand, in order that they maintain their objectivity.

While doing an observation, try to be a 'fly on the wall', so you can glean objective information. Even if the child does something that requires adult intervention, you must resist the temptation to become involved – leave it to your colleagues to sort out the problem, but continue making notes on what's happening. You can then use the information to plan specific targets, strategies and methods to support the child's progress.

Figure 5.2 provides an example of a Focused Observation Form.

There's a blank photocopiable version of the form on page 107.

Assessments

Our society supports a veritable industry of assessments, starting almost from a child's birth, with charts, records, checklists and so on! While you may feel we've gone totally overboard with it all, be careful not to throw out the baby with the bathwater – assessments do have a valuable place in helping us to focus on a child's achievements and areas of need. The skill comes in selecting the appropriate assessment for the particular situation and using its results to plan effectively for the child's support.

Speaking very broadly there are two basic types of assessment: standardised and individualised.

Standardised assessments

These are the commercially available 'tests' or assessments produced and validated by official bodies. They usually become available for use only after much research, careful design and planning, piloting within the target population,

Figure 5.2 An example of a completed Focused Observation Form

Focused Observation Form

Child's name: Una Kelly   **Date of birth:** 22.01.00

Date and time of observation: 16.06.04;   **Observer:** Clare Moore
10.45–11.00

Una alone at water play, pours water from cup into bowl; mumbling to herself. Goes to sink and fills cup with water, returns to water tray and pours water into watermill. Tries to stop water leaving watermill; gets frustrated ('naughty toy'); leaves water play. Goes to model making (no place free); stands beside Susan, watches her making model. 'Let me try' – Susan refuses. Una tries to snatch Susan's glue brush; girls tussle and Una slaps Susan's hand; Susan cries and goes to J.W. Una sits on Susan's seat and smashes Susan's model. J.W. intervenes & asks why she hit Susan; Una denies it; J.W. tells Una to leave model-making area. Una goes to Home Corner and plays with doll. Asks to join other children's game; they refuse. Una cuddles doll alone in corner.

Area of learning: Personal and social development

Learning targets:

1. Waiting to take turn if activities not yet available.

2. Being gentle, i.e. controlling urge to hit, etc.

3.

Strategies:

1. Agree system with Una for rewards for each time she waits to take her turn.

2. Plan programme with rewards for specific time-spans spent with specified positive behaviour.

3.

critical analysis of the results, application of statistics to ensure the results are significant and can be correlated across the target population, and validation by the appropriate organisations (which can include, for example, government departments, university departments, commercial and private establishments, or any combination of these).

For our purposes, what we're left with, after all of the above, is a test, assessment, checklist, baseline or set of criteria that we can use to judge the progress of a child compared with their national (and sometimes even international) peer group. By applying the assessment, we can see what areas of strength the child has and what skills they need to develop, in relation to the other children of their age across the country.

There are pros and cons to standardised assessments, particularly in the early years sector. They can give you an overview of the child's development in a broad sense, but they don't give you a picture of the child's progress in relation to themselves or their recent developmental history. For example, Una may be delayed linguistically for her age, according to a standardised language assessment, but she may have made amazing progress with her language development over the last six months, a fact which won't be reflected in the test (unless it's a repeat of one done earlier in the year – but be wary of 'over-testing' very young children).

If you and your colleagues decide to use a standardised assessment, make sure it's a reliable test, has been validated by a body or organisation with the highest reputation, and is relevant and appropriate to the area of the child's development that you're hoping to measure. Above all, don't use it every five minutes to 'check up' on the child's progress – comparative results are only useful after retests done much later.

Individualised assessments

These are assessments designed with a smaller population in mind and are more 'localised' and specific to the child being assessed. So, for example, any baseline assessments or checklists used by your setting can be classed as individualised because they measure a child's achievements in relation to their peer group within your setting, within the neighbourhood and against the child's own development. They can give you a much clearer picture of specific areas of need, as well as areas of achievement, thereby helping you to plan for a focus or target which is relevant to a particular child.

Your LEA may have its own assessments or checklists, and these will have been designed with the local population in mind. For example, there wouldn't be much point in trying to assess the language development of a child from an inner London area using vocabulary and concepts based on countryside and rural experiences. Use assessments that are available locally and if you think they need to be adapted to make them a little more appropriate to your situation, you can do this without skewing any results. The beauty of individualised assessments is that they measure the child against themselves, within their own context.

If you're not sure which assessments to use, ask for help in deciding. Your Area SENCO will be able to advise, and your Early Years Learning Support Service (EYLSS) will give you help and information. You could also ask your local educational psychologist (EP) to make some suggestions. But the most important thing is that your choice of assessment is relevant to your children and gives a fair and useful picture of their progress.

Examples of work

Sometimes a child's difficulties are reflected in their work in the setting. By this I mean the things produced during activities, such as, for example, a painting, some writing, a model, a photograph you take of them when they're presenting behaviour which illustrates a particular difficulty.

If you feel that something connected with the child or created by the child highlights your concerns, keep it in the child's file. If you need to move to Early Years Action Plus, or even Statutory Assessment, it may prove very important as part of your body of evidence.

CASE STUDY

Rebecca, aged 4, was displaying very disturbing behaviour almost every day in the setting. She was being aggressive, both physically and verbally, towards the other children. Practitioners saw her on two occasions performing inappropriate and mature sexual acts on a doll in the Home Corner during solitary play. Eventually the educational psychologist became involved.

One day Rebecca produced a drawing that clearly illustrated male genitalia alongside a female figure. When her key worker asked her what her picture was about she said, 'It's me and Grandad doing our secret.' Rebecca then went on to disclose what seemed to be sexual abuse by her grandfather.

Investigations by child protection officers found this to be the case and Rebecca's grandfather was eventually convicted and jailed. Her picture was used as evidence in drawing up the case for the prosecution (in view of her tender age, she didn't testify in court, but was interviewed by the child protection officers).

The educational psychologist also decided that the abuse was probably at the root of Rebecca's negative behaviour, and indeed after her grandfather was removed from the situation, she became a different child: much happier, relaxed and very social.

Profiles

Every child in an early years setting should have a Profile – a record of their achievements, skills and areas of need – and children with additional needs are no different. Their Profile should show their development and achievements in the six areas of learning of the Foundation Stage curriculum:

- personal, social and emotional development (PSE)

- communication, language and literacy (CLL)

- mathematical development (MD)

- knowledge and understanding of the world (KUW)

- physical development (PD)

- creative development (CD).

There's no need to transfer all the information on an IEP to the Profile – you'll only be wasting time duplicating data and the two documents should complement each other anyway – but a note such as 'See IEP', where necessary, should be enough. It's as crucial to keep the Profile up to date as it is the other records. It gives the wider picture of the child's development and should reflect and support the content of the more focused IEP.

Remember – it isn't your job as SENCO to keep a child's records up to date (unless you're their primary practitioner). Your role is to make sure the practitioners working with the child monitor and update the files regularly.

Checklists

You can go on forever trying to select a checklist, ranging from commercially produced versions, to downloaded Internet versions, to your own version designed within the setting. Which checklists you choose for your setting is entirely up to you, but the choice should be made by everybody. After all, it's everybody who'll be using them, so colleagues must be comfortable with them.

In relation to a child with additional needs, you might find the following questions useful when thinking of drawing up a checklist for your setting. Each section ties in with one of the areas of need as outlined in the *SEN Code of Practice*.

Communication and interaction

Watch for the little one who:

- hardly ever talks or does not talk at all;

- stammers or has slow speech, but understands what you say to them, and what they say makes sense;

- has delayed or distorted speech that's difficult to understand;

- has normal speech but what they say may be odd or inappropriate in context;

- has normal speech but doesn't seem to understand what you say to them and/or doesn't respond appropriately to other people;

- speaks at inappropriate times or makes inappropriate remarks;

- laughs very loudly or for too long;

- finds it hard to take turns during conversations and/or has poor conversational skills;

- has ritualistic or obsessive behaviours or habits;

- has problems communicating through speech and/or other forms of language;

- can't use appropriate verbal and/or non-verbal language;

- doesn't react 'normally' in social situations or avoids social situations;

- behaves passively and has little or no initiative or curiosity;

- seems to be unaware of other people and their needs or emotions;

- has unusual voice tone, uses bizarre language and/or ritualistic phrases such as advertisement jingles or slogans.

Cognition and learning

Look out for the child who:

- has poor scores on assessments or profiles compared with the other children of the same age in their group;

- has markedly lower levels of development (in all or specific areas) and play than those of the other children;

- finds difficulty in developing their skills, especially in communication and interaction, literacy and numeracy;

- can't deal with abstract ideas and/or generalise concepts from personal experience (older children);

- makes little or no progress in spite of involvement in the nursery curriculum;

- doesn't achieve their set targets;

- makes little or no progress despite your differentiated curriculum.

Behavioural, emotional and social development

Watch for the child who:

- is verbally and/or physically aggressive with other children and/or adults;

- is introverted or withdrawn, or seems troubled and worried;

- is loud and inappropriately outgoing;
- behaves inappropriately for their chronological age;
- has strange or socially inappropriate behaviour;
- does things that may cause self-injury;
- can't stay on task, despite support and encouragement from an adult;
- regularly disrupts the routine;
- doesn't make progress;
- is often absent;
- has bouts of uncooperative behaviour;
- behaves unpredictably and/or has erratic attitudes to learning;
- shows little interest in activities and games;
- seems to be over-dependent on adults;
- seems to be hyperactive;
- can't play with other children, or play with them 'normally';
- can't share or take turns with toys and equipment;
- shows poor or no conversational skills.

Sensory and/or physical

See if the child:

- has difficulty in coordinating their hands and feet;
- experiences problems in balancing;
- has poor gross and/or fine motor skills;
- moves around clumsily.

They may have visual difficulties if they:

- hold books and objects close to their face to look at them;
- always sit at the front for stories or television and then strain to look at the book or TV;
- bang into or trip over objects;
- have a lack of confidence when moving around the room and/or show anxiety about banging into things;
- find difficulty in focusing on an object or have problems in eye tracking;

- have difficulty in doing activities that require visual skills and/or have difficulty with hand–eye coordination;

- have unusual eye movements such as roving or 'trembling' of the eyeball;

- display abnormal social interaction or autistic-type behaviours;

- hold their head in an unusual position;

- display eye poking, rocking or other 'blindisms'.

They may have hearing difficulties if they:

- concentrate intensively on the faces and body gestures of the adults in the setting;

- either don't follow instructions, follow instructions only sometimes and/or follow instructions wrongly;

- don't respond to their name, especially if you call them from behind;

- watch the other children before doing an action, and then copy the others;

- appear to need more visual input and support during activities than the other children in the group;

- behave inappropriately or seem to be frustrated without any apparent cause;

- don't react to loud or unexpected noises;

- shout or talk too loudly without realising it;

- have delayed speech or speech that's difficult to understand;

- change their voice tone while they're speaking;

- have difficulty doing activities that require listening skills;

- have discharges from their ear(s), which don't seem to clear up or which occur quite frequently;

- tilt their head when listening to stories, instructions and so on;

- appear to be in a world of their own or showing autistic-type behaviours.

These checklists are not to be interpreted as a 'diagnosis' or way of labelling a child. Use them only to give yourself an indication of which areas of development you might need to focus on for supporting the child most effectively.

Individual Education Plans (IEPs)

IEPs are explored in greater detail in Chapter 4. However, here we have a quick reminder of the acronym that characterises the targets of IEPs:

SMART:

- Specific – written concisely so everybody knows exactly **what** the child's aims are

- Measurable – so everybody knows exactly **when** the aims have been achieved

- Achievable – so everybody knows the targets **can** be reached and **how** the child will do this

- Recorded – so everybody knows the **progress** being made

- Time-defined – so everybody knows **by when** (i.e. the date) the targets should be achieved.

Let's have a look of the example IEP from Chapter 4 in terms of **SMART** (Figure 5.3).

Notice that Harry's targets are written in *Specific* terms, making his aims quite clear. The criteria for success outline exactly how achievements will be *Measurable*. The targets are *Achievable* because they've been chosen as the next stage on from Harry's current strengths. That the information is *Recorded* on the IEP form satisfies this requirement. The 'deadline' date shows that Harry's targets are *Time-defined*.

The IEPs are probably your most important records and getting them right is crucial. The reason why is discussed in the section *Records as evidence* below.

IEP/review summaries

To save you rummaging through every child's file to jog your memory about what stage they've reached, you could have a Summary Sheet similar to the one shown in Figure 5.4.

It's a quick reference to what's happening over any three-monthly/termly period. Make sure that it's

- accessible to all staff;

- displayed somewhere private and confidential;

- updated regularly – pop the dates and data on straight after each review.

RECORDS AS EVIDENCE

The value placed on the records of a child with additional needs can't be rated too highly. They're not just another set of files from which the authorities can draw statistics for the government returns. They're the hard evidence of the child's achievements, development and continuing areas of need. It's vital that everybody in your setting places great store by the records, not least because they may be your key to accessing further support for the child should they need it.

Figure 5.3   *Making an IEP SMART*

Individual Education Plan

Child's name: Harry Jones   **DOB:** 29.03.00

Date IEP implemented: 13.01.04   **Code of Practice level:** E Y Action

Areas of strength: Harry enjoys books; he paints excellent pictures.

Areas of difficulty: Harry has difficulty with early number work. He has hearing problems – he's got grommets; he regularly attends the ear nose & throat department at the hospital.

Targets to be reached by: 8.04.03

1)   Harry will be able to count from 1 to 4 using apparatus.

2)   Harry will be able to recognise and name 1 to 4 when shown in written form.

3)   Harry will be able to write any numeral from 1 to 4 on request.

Criteria for success:

1)   Harry will count from 1 to 4 using four different types of apparatus, 4 times out of 5.

2)   Harry will recognise and name 1, 2 , 3 or 4 in written form in a variety of places, 4 times out of 5.

3)   Harry will correctly write a requested numeral from 1 to 4, 4 times out of 5.

Teaching methods: initially in a one-to-one situation in the quiet area; then in the main nursery areas to use counting displays, posters, name tags, etc.

Staff involved: Mrs Smith, early years teacher; Mrs Scott, nursery nurse; Mrs Jones, mother, to work at home.

Frequency of programme: twice daily (morning and afternoon) for a maximum of ten minutes, five days per week; once per evening at home when possible.

Equipment/Apparatus: cubes, counters, plastic sorting shapes, any appropriate counting apparatus of Harry's choice, paper, pencils and felt-tip pens.

Date of next review: 9.04.04

To be attended by Mrs Smith, Mrs Scott & Mrs Jones.

Figure 5.4 **Example Summary Sheet**

IEP/Review Summary Sheet

Summary Year: 2004–2005

1 Jan–31 March 2004				
Child's name	**Code of Practice level**	**IEP no. & date implemented**	**Last review date & outcome**	**Next review due**
Harry Jones	EY Action	No. 1 13.01.04	Not applicable yet	9.04.04
John Davies	EY Action	No. 3 12.01.04	9.04.04 Move to EYA+	21.05.04
Sadie Scott	EY Action Plus	No. 3 10.12.03	21.03.04 Refer for Statutory Assessment	1.05.04
1 April–30 June 2004				
1 July–30 September 2004				
1 October–31 December 2004				

You might now be thinking, *What's this woman talking about?* It's very simple. If a child moves to Early Years Action Plus and/or Statutory Assessment, their records will form the basis on which decisions will be made that affect provision for the child. It's clear from this how crucially important it is to have **accurate** and **continuous** records. Let's see what I *am* talking about!

Early Years Action Plus

As we've seen, this is the level of the *SEN Code of Practice* where you ask for the help and advice of an outside agent. Remember – it's possible (even likely) that the agent won't know your little one from Adam. They have to rely on the information you give them to build up a picture of the child's achievements and difficulties. It could have taken anything up to a year for you to reach this stage, so an accurate record of what was happening a year ago, in the interim and very recently, is needed. Suppose the child is four years old. If it has taken one year to reach Early Years Action Plus, that's a quarter of their entire lifespan – quite a daunting thought. The agent's support (type, level, quantity, etc.) will be influenced by what's in your records, so make them good ones!

Statutory Assessment

If the child moves to Statutory Assessment, the LEA's going to ask you for all the child's records. But, crucially, they're going to ask you to show:

- whether you consulted outside agents;
- whether you took the advice of the outside agents;
- how you implemented that advice;
- what form the liaison between yourselves and the outside agents took.

If you present the LEA with faulty, 'spotty', inaccurate and/or incomplete records, they may decide there's insufficient evidence of SEN. You'll have poured down the drain in one go all the time, effort, and commitment, and, what's worse, you may delay the child's entitlements being met. This isn't a melodramatic view – it's what can happen through poor administration. We owe it to the children not to let that happen.

SUMMARY

The **key points** covered in this chapter were:

- The crucial importance of setting up and maintaining records.
- The role of the SENCO regarding records.
- The different types of records: observations, assessments, examples of work, profiles and checklists, IEPs, IEP/review summaries.
- Records as evidence.

Continuous Observation Form

Date	Observation	Area of learning	Planning	Observer

Focused Observation Form

Child's name: Date of birth:

Date & time of observation: Observer:

Area of learning:

Learning targets:

Strategies:

IEP/Review Summary Sheet

Summary Year: _____

Child's name	Code of Practice level	IEP no. & date implemented	Last review date & outcome	Next review due

Chapter 6

A parent thing – maintaining a collaborative partnership

The **key points** covered in this chapter are:

- Involving the parents at various levels.

- Designing and using Play Plans.

- Parent Partnership Services.

- Parents with additional needs.

- Documentation for parents.

INTRODUCTION

Here we'll look at your role in ensuring that the parents are supported at all levels of involvement in the special educational needs (SEN) process. We'll explore your duties with regard to Parent Partnership Services (PPS) and also the issues involved when the parents themselves have additional needs, and how you can ensure that they're included in the process, despite their difficulties.

INVOLVING THE PARENTS

Parents of children with additional needs have the right to become involved from your earliest concerns and, as SENCO, you have a major responsibility to ensure this happens.

There are various degrees of parental involvement, depending on which level of the *SEN Code of Practice* we're talking about. It can be, for example:

- having a quick word at pick-up time about the day's events;

- keeping a home/setting diary (daily or weekly);

- collaborating on Play Plans;

- sharing Individual Education Plans (IEPs);

- discussing the way forward via reviews.

SOME PRACTICALITIES OF PARENTAL INVOLVEMENT

- If the child's difficulties have only recently been identified, the parents might be going through a grieving process, so be sensitive to their feelings. They're likely to be less stressed if the child's problem was identified at birth, for example Down's syndrome, since they'll have had three or four years to come to terms with the situation.

- Be prepared for a variety of reactions: disbelief, denial, grief, self-blame, even aggression. There is also 'Thank goodness, someone's believed me and given it a name!' There can be over-protection and extreme anxiety. Understand and make allowances for any of these.

- Listen to the parents, giving them time to talk; but use this approach wisely – you and the other children also have needs, so make sure they are met too.

- Give the parents encouragement and positive feedback about their child's progress, efforts, positive behaviour and achieved targets. They need something positive to hang on to – even something like 'Laura's tried very hard today, Mrs Jones – we're really pleased with her'.

- Don't tell them that the child has achieved something unless they really have – it's vitally important to be truthful.

- Always tell parents about any discussions that take place if an outside agent 'pops in' to talk to you and the parents weren't present.

- Without being patronising, give them credit for any support or follow-up work they do at home. You'll reduce their sense of isolation and they'll know that they're *doing* something for their child and doing it well.

- Be a mutual support group. The parents know how their child reacts to things at home; you know how they react in the setting. Sharing this information will give all of you a resource of knowledge about the child that you can use in your planning.

- Give the parents the contact details of relevant societies, associations, self-help groups, etc., which provide another strand of support that they may welcome.

- Ask them everything you want to know about their child. They're the experts on the child and can be a fount of information that you can exploit.

- If the parents are following a Play Plan, emphasise that as soon as the child shows any boredom, distraction or distress, they should stop doing the activity. If the child is forced to continue, they won't enjoy the activity, therefore they won't gain anything from it and they may even turn against it, so defeating your whole aim.

- If the parents aren't familiar with the songs, rhymes and games you use in the setting, invite them to sit in on a few sessions at drop-off or collection time. They will very quickly pick up the technique.

ACTIVITY REPORTS

Encourage the child's key worker to set up a home/setting activity report to tell the parents about:

- the child's current target;

- the games and activities being used to achieve the target;

- the child's progress towards achieving the target (in positive terms, e.g. 'Andrew can identify his name card from among five others', not 'Andrew still can't say what sound his name begins with');

- how the child keeps their own records (e.g. Andrew might have his own book of stickers or a chart with balloons to colour in).

Decide between yourselves how often to send the report back and forth. Some settings choose a daily report, others do it on a weekly basis. Figure 6.1 shows an example of a completed Weekly Activity Report. Depending on the child's achievement level, you can help them complete the form, or fill it in for them, writing what they tell you.

There's a blank photocopiable version of the form on page 126. You can easily adapt it to a Daily Activity Report, and change it in other ways to suit your particular needs.

PLAY PLANS

A Play Plan is a very effective method of involving the parents in doing support and follow-up work with the child at home. The targets of a Play Plan are linked with those of the child's Differentiated Learning Plan (DLP) or IEP, and incorporate games, activities and play sessions that will reinforce your teaching points. It's a good way of sharing information about the child's progress and also lets the child see that you and their parents are working together to support them.

CASE STUDY

Cindy has Down's syndrome and some accompanying learning difficulties. She's learning her colours, particularly red and green (other colours will be added later). Her Mum and the early years practitioner developed a Play Plan aimed at getting Cindy to recognise and name the two colours correctly whenever she was asked. The first part of the Play Plan states what Cindy's targets are and how her Mum will help her work towards them. The second section is for Cindy's Mum to make a record of her progress. Figure 6.2 shows the completed Play Plan.

Figure 6.1 An example of a completed Weekly Activity Report

Weekly Activity Report

My name is Andrew Johnson

Today is Friday 13 March 2004

I'm trying to fasten my coat buttons all by myself

and listen to stories quietly

This week I played with the button-fastening game, the dressing up box, the teddies

and the books in the story corner, the computer and the stories on the tape recorder

Now I can fasten 2 buttons on my coat

and listen quietly for three minutes

This week I filled in five balloons on my clown chart

Figure 6.2   **An example of a Play Plan for home/setting liason**

Play Plan for <u>Cindy Davies</u>   and <u>Cindy's Mum</u>

<u>Cindy</u>   will play these games to help <u>Cindy to recognise red</u>

<u>and green and to say their names</u>   :

Sorting and naming all the red things she can find, followed by green things when she knows red very well.

Painting and potato printing using red first, then green when she knows red.

Sorting and matching all the red shapes, then the green ones.

Naming red things that she takes out of the feely bag; then the green ones.

<u>Begin by</u>

looking at lots of red things (never mind about green at first); help Cindy to sort out all her red clothes (socks, jumpers, hat, etc.); say the word 'red' each time and encourage Cindy to repeat it. Then ask 'What colour is this?' – if Cindy needs to be reminded, say 'red' again.

Here's what _____<u>Cindy</u>_____ did:

Tuesday 4 May. Cindy seemed to mix up the colour with the clothes at first – she'd say Sock when I asked what colour it was, but then she'd say Red after I said it.

Wednesday 5 May. Cindy spotted her dad's red rugby shirt and shouted Red.

Thursday 6 May. We started looking at green today. She seems to be getting the hang of it. She pointed to my mug and said Green. Her older sister's helping her too.

Saturday 8 May. Cindy can tell you red or green almost every time you ask, no matter what you point to. I think she's ready to move on to the next colours.

Date when this Play Plan was finished at home: **<u>Sunday 9 May</u>**

There's a blank photocopiable Play Plan Form on page 127. You can adapt it to suit your own requirements or use it as it stands.

PARENT PARTNERSHIP SERVICES

All Local Education Authorities (LEAs) have a legal obligation to make arrangements for a Parent Partnership Service (PPS) with the aim of ensuring that the parents of a child with additional needs receive the support, advice, help and information that they're entitled to. The LEA doesn't have to provide the PPS themselves – they may prefer to commission outside providers to offer the service and this is perfectly acceptable. Their obligation is to ensure the parents can access the service easily. When they establish the PPS, they should make arrangements for the involvement of the voluntary sector and organisations, which can advise about specific areas of need, and give relevant and appropriate support to the parents.

As SENCO, it's one of your duties to tell the child's parents about the PPS, what it offers and how they can access it. Your LEA should have provided you with all the paperwork, information, leaflets and brochures, contact details, etc. that you need. If you don't have this documentation, contact the SEN department of your education offices and ask for everything they have about their PPS. Alternatively, ask your Area SENCO where you can access the information.

The main function of the PPS is to help, advise and support the parents of children with special educational needs. This includes liaison between parents and practitioners if there are difficulties between home and the setting. By handling such situations sensitively, the PPS can help prevent difficulties from developing into disagreements.

The *SEN Code of Practice* outlines the minimum standards that the PPS should meet. As SENCO you'll be in a strong position if you're aware of these standards, since you can check that your LEA does indeed support your parents through its PPS. The standards are as follows:

- the provision of a range of flexible services including their best endeavours to provide access to an Independent Parental Supporter for all parents who want one

- that practical support is offered to parents, either individually or in groups, to help them in their discussions with schools, LEAs and other statutory agencies

- that parents (including all those with parental responsibility for the child) are provided with accurate, neutral information on their rights, roles and responsibilities within the SEN process, and on the wide range of options that are available for their children's education

- that parents are informed about other agencies, such as Health Services, Social Services and voluntary organisations, which can offer information and advice about their child's particular SEN. This may be particularly important at the time the LEA issues a proposed statement

- that, where appropriate and in conjunction with their parents, the ascertainable views and wishes of the child are sought and taken into consideration

- that information about the available services is published widely in the area using a variety of means

- the provision of neutral, accurate information for parents on all SEN procedures as set out in SEN legislation and the SEN Code of Practice

- the interpretation of information published by schools, LEAs and othe bodies interested in SEN

- that a wide range of information for parents is available in community languages, and to parents who may not be able to gain access to information through conventional means

- that advice on special educational needs procedures is made available to parents through information, support and training

- they use their best endeavours to recruit sufficient Independent Parental Supporters to meet the needs of parents in their area, including arrangements for appropriate training, ensuring that they are kept up to date with all relevant aspects of SEN policy and procedures so that they can fulfil their role effectively

- that training on good communication and relationships with parents is made available to teachers, governors and staff in SEN sections of the LEA

- they work with schools, LEA officers, and other agencies to help them develop positive relationships with parents

- they establish and maintain links with voluntary organisations

- that parents' views are heard and understood, and inform and influence the development of local SEN policy and practice

- the regular review of the effectiveness of the service they provide, for instance by seeking feedback from users.

(*Special Educational Needs Code of Practice*, DfES, 2001, 2:21)

PARENTS WITH ADDITIONAL NEEDS

Some parents of children with SEN may have additional needs themselves. In this case, you must make sure that your cooperation and support are sensitive, understanding and respectful. Bear in mind that they may have had unhappy educational experiences as children themselves and could be feeling extremely threatened by the situation they're in. They may be anxious that their child is going to come up against the same negative attitudes they did themselves. As SENCO you must do everything you can to reassure them. Let them see how times have changed by adopting a positive, warm and supportive approach, and by encouraging their involvement in an appropriate way.

You need to be aware of and sensitive to the parents' perspective of the situation, which could be very different from yours, simply because of their differing needs. It's essential that you work together to find common ground for making sure the child receives the support and help they're entitled to from home/setting collaboration. Try to see things from the parents' point of view and go forward from that position.

Parents' differing needs can be varied – for example, learning difficulties, a disability, communication or linguistic difficulties. These needs should be respected, and you must make sure that the parents receive the same standard of courtesy and support as all the parents do. If, for example, they'd like to bring another family member to meetings to help and support them, then you should be very willing for this to happen; if they'd like to have the support of a translator, whether of another language or another system of communication for the same reasons, then, again, be flexible enough to welcome this.

Parents with additional needs may find it difficult to attend your meetings because of commitments connected with their own needs. For example, a parent with a long-term medical condition may have to attend hospital appointments during your allocated review times. You should be flexible in situations like this and offer alternative appointments, tying in where you can with the parents' commitments.

CASE STUDY

Marian's son Billy is four and attends his local nursery, aiming to transfer to the infant school next term. Billy is a hearing child and he is working on an IEP that's targeting his language and communication skills. Marian is profoundly deaf and communicates by using British Sign Language (BSL). At IEP planning sessions and IEP reviews, Marian needs the help of a signing interpreter. By coincidence, the head of the nursery is a qualified and experienced teacher of the deaf, who uses BSL proficiently. She joins the members of Billy's team at their meetings to provide the interpretation that Marian and the others need, to communicate effectively.

> **CASE STUDY**
>
> Jade's mum, Louise, has learning difficulties and attended a (segregated) special school herself. Fortunately, her school career was very happy and she doesn't have any reservations about Jade going through the SEN process. Jade also has learning difficulties and, at six, is working towards many of the Foundation Stage goals. Louise sometimes finds it hard to understand the finer details of the planning and decision making for Jade, so comes to the meetings and reviews with her own Mum, Barbara. Together they take a full and active part in planning Jade's IEPs, and Barbara helps with the home sessions as well.

RECORDS AND DOCUMENTATION

In earlier chapters, we've seen some examples of record keeping and documentation that could form part of the child's folio. All documentation regarding the child should be clear, concise and easy to understand, and, above all, freely available to the parents. Let them know that you're willing to talk them through the documentation about their child. They must feel relaxed and comfortable enough to ask you to explain anything they don't understand.

Most parents are keen and positive about becoming involved in their child's programmes and action plans. If they lack confidence a little about becoming involved and/or their ability to support their child, let them see from the Play Plans, IEPs and other records that we're not talking about rocket science. These are all good, down-to-earth, practical tactics, shared and tried until the 'magic formula' is discovered – the key to giving the child that starting point to achievement.

Some parents, however, choose not to become involved with the work that you're doing with their child, and in that case you must make sure that the child's support is rock solid within the setting. This choice by the parents doesn't mean that you can ignore them, or that you don't need to keep them updated about their child's progress. Through letters, reports and, where possible, personal contact, you should continue to inform them of how you're helping their child.

In this section, there are a few examples of letters you can send to parents who, for whatever reason, haven't kept in touch with you, haven't attended contact sessions/meetings or haven't become involved with their child's programmes. As always, these letters are photocopiable, but you can use them as a framework to formulate your own letters in a style and with language more appropriate to your parents.

Always make photocopies of any letters and documentation you send home, particularly if the child's parents are uncooperative or uninvolved, and keep the copies in the child's file. Also, send your letters and documents by post, getting proof of posting. Sadly, you may have to prove at some stage that you did indeed try to keep the parents closely involved with what you're doing, and these copies and proof of posting may be your only 'evidence'.

Expressing concern and Differentiated Learning Plans

The letter on page 120 can be sent to the child's parents if they haven't been able to come and discuss with you your concerns about their child.

Early Years Action

Use the letter on page 121 to inform parents when you've decided to move the child to Early Years Action.

You can send the letter on page 122 if the parents didn't accept your invitation to come and discuss their child's progress.

The letter on page 123 can be sent if you're still having little or no contact with the parents, and the IEP review is approaching.

If the parents didn't attend the IEP review, you can follow up with the letter on page 124, providing the decision at the review was to continue at Early Years Action.

Early Years Action Plus

If you decided at the review that the child should move to Early Years Action Plus, it's imperative that you inform their parents immediately – don't refer the child to any outside agent until you've spoken to the parents. The letter on page 125 may be appropriate.

If this still doesn't do the trick, don't battle along on your own any longer. GET ADVICE! There are various options you can take, depending on the child's circumstances.

- Contact your Area SENCO and discuss how to find a way forward.

- Speak to the PPS, respecting the parents' confidentiality, and ask their advice. They should be able to offer you some practical suggestions.

- If a social worker is involved with the family, you could ask them to speak to the parents about the potential referral to an outside agent.

- The health visitor may be willing to pay a visit and try to persuade the parents to become involved, or at least give you permission to refer. Don't speak to them, however, unless they're already involved with the family – calling them in 'cold' goes against the spirit of the *SEN Code of Practice*.

- Is there a practitioner in the setting who's closer to the parent(s) and who they might be more willing to speak to?

- Is only one parent resisting your invitations? Perhaps the other can become involved and able to offer support.

At the end of the day, you still need to have the willing cooperation and support of the child's parents, so try to keep the situation as positive and amicable as possible. Calling in 'the heavy mob' may force the parents to face the situation, but then what? You're certainly not going to have a pleasant working relationship afterwards. Try to meet them on their terms – remember they may be very frightened, very threatened, even fearful that you're going to take their child away from them – and keep reassuring them that you're on their side. The ultimate goal for all of you is the child's progress, welfare and development; you're batting on the same team, so be persistent in your support of the parents, too, and hopefully it will all come right in the end.

SUMMARY

The **key points** covered in this chapter were:

- Involving the parents at various levels.

- Designing and using Play Plans.

- Parent Partnership Services.

- Parents with additional needs.

- Documentation for parents.

Dear

I am sorry that you were not able to come to see me about
_____ on _____.

As you know, we have a few concerns about _____'s
progress and we're now going to plan his/her activities here to
help him/her develop as well as possible.

I'm enclosing a copy of _____'s Differentiated
Learning Plan, which shows what we hope to do with
_____ over the next few weeks.

I hope you'll be able to call in soon and talk about
_____'s progress, and how you think we might be able
to help him/her in other ways. Perhaps when you come to collect
_____, you could have a short chat with me about their
Learning Plan.

Best wishes,

Dear

I am sorry that you weren't able to come to the meeting about
_____ 's progress on _____.

We are still concerned about his/her progress and have decided to take Early Years Action. This means that we will plan his/her activities and work here, with targets for him/her to achieve over a few weeks.

If you'd like to talk to me about this, feel free to come and see me when you drop off or collect _____ any day. Or, if you'd like to arrange a meeting, just let me know and we can fix a time to suit you.

Best wishes,

Dear

I am sorry that we haven't been able to get together to talk about
_____ 's progress.

As you know, we're still planning _____ 's work to help
him/her to achieve his/her targets. We hope very much that you'll
be able to help us with the planning and so I'd like to ask you to
call in to see me on _____ at _____. If this
isn't convenient, let me know and we can agree a better time.

In the meantime I enclose a copy of _____ 's latest
Individual Education Plan. You can see how well _____
is doing and how pleased we are with him/her.

If you'd like to talk to us about the Plan, I'll be delighted to go
through it with you when you come on _____.

Best wishes,

Dear

As you know, _____ has been following an Individual Education Plan here for the last six weeks.

It's now time to have a look at _____ 's progress and make sure that we're still helping him/her properly.

We're going to talk about the Plan on _____ at _____ to decide whether it's working and whether we need to change anything on it.

We hope very much that you'll be able to join us and help us to make the next decision about the best ways of helping _____.

If the time above isn't good for you, but you can manage to come to a meeting on another date, please let me know and we'll get together then.

Best wishes,

Dear

I am sorry that you weren't able to join us when we met to discuss
_____ 's Individual Education Plan. We would very
much have liked you to tell us how you feel about
_____ 's progress.

I enclose a copy of the Review Form, which shows you what we
decided. If you'd like to talk about this with me, feel free to call
in at any time to suit you.

_____ seems to be doing very well and we're pleased
with his/her progress. We hope you'll be pleased too.

Best wishes,

Dear

I am sorry that you weren't able to join us when we met to discuss
_____ 's progress. I enclose a copy of the Review Form,
which shows you what we decided.

We really need to talk with you about _____'s
progress, and so I hope I shall be able to see you when you drop
_____ off or collect him/her one day this week. It
won't take us very long, so I'll try to catch you before you leave.
Thank you.

Best wishes,

Weekly Activity Report

My name is _____

Today is _____

I'm trying to _____

and _____

This week I played with _____

and _____

Now I can _____

and _____

This week I _____

Play Plan

Play Plan for .... and ....

.... will play these games to help ....

.... :

Begin by

Here's what .... did:

Date when this Play Plan was finished at home: ....

Coming together – the teamwork approach

The **key points** covered in this chapter are:

- The rationale behind the referral.

- The why, who and what of outside agency involvement.

- The child – the central character in the referral.

INTRODUCTION

The original plans didn't work; the child's still causing concern; it's time to take further action – Early Years Action Plus, characterised by requesting outside agents to share with you their more specialised knowledge and experience. Here we'll have a look at the process in more detail.

THE RATIONALE BEHIND THE REFERRAL

There's no need for anxiety either by you as SENCO, or by your colleagues, when you reach the point of referring a child to an outside agent. It's the next logical step in the graduated approach of supporting the child. So what's it all about? Let's explore the reasons.

THE WHY, WHO AND WHAT OF OUTSIDE AGENCY INVOLVEMENT

Why involve outside agents?

Don't know why you've been sent here – we don't have special needs in this school. Worked here for thirty years and never needed help yet.

These were the words I was greeted with on my first visit to a tiny primary school in the North Yorkshire dales, almost twenty years ago. The whole concept of the teamwork approach was new and very daunting to many professionals. The comment was made by a head teacher whose practices had never before been questioned, and who felt very threatened by the 'slip of a lass' who was sent to her school to support a child with recognised needs. Hopefully we've come a long way from that, and now practitioners in training learn from the outset the value and necessity of working as a team.

That head teacher's professional self-esteem was low. She felt deskilled, unsuccessful and challenged. Sadly, there are still practitioners who perceive a decision to ask for outside help as a negative judgement on them, that somehow they've 'failed' to support a child. As SENCO, you play a crucial role in ensuring your colleagues don't develop these feelings and perceptions.

You usually call an outside agent in to support a child because they have more specialised experience, skills and expertise in specific areas of the child's development than can be offered by the practitioners in your setting. This isn't to say that the experience and expertise within your setting is of less value – far from it. As professionals, you and your colleagues have a wide-ranging expertise in mainstream early years practice. It's important to acknowledge this and recognise the immense value it has in the successful planning for and support of the child with additional needs. You have an overview of the usual milestones of child development, and are therefore in a superb position to identify a child who doesn't pass them at an appropriate time, or in an appropriate way. It's the information about the child, based on your knowledge and expertise, that you hand over to the outside agent.

You can use an analogy of a joiner and a cabinet-maker: both create beautiful things with wood using similar skills; if you needed a staircase, you'd probably ask the joiner; if you needed intricately carved spindles on it, you'd ask the cabinet-maker. Neither craftsman is 'better' than the other – their expertise is simply different. It's the same with our profession. Seen in this context, it's crucial that we peel back any false pride we may have, and overcome any feelings of inadequacy or threat. We must realise the implications on the child of not calling in an outside agent when one is needed. We must have the integrity to accept our professional limitations and ask for help.

You'll find more details about how you actually ask for this help, how you refer a child to an outside agent, on page 72.

● Who are the outside agents?

In Chapter 4 (page 70) there's a sort of 'Who's Who' of outside agents, the external professionals you'd be most likely to ask for help. Figure 7.1 summarises this. The *Special Educational Needs (SEN) Code of Practice* gives four important principles for a successful inter-agency partnership:

- early identification
- continual engagement with the child and parents
- focused intervention
- dissemination of effective approaches and techniques.[1]

Early identification

It's unarguable that early identification of any difficulty is crucial, particularly when talking about early years children with additional needs. For this reason, you're in the front line when it comes to spotting a child whose progress is causing concern. Even if you can't identify the specific difficulty, you know from the child's performance relative to the rest of their peer group that there's something you need to investigate, and you're in the best position to call for specialised help early on. Time wasted is the child's time lost, so the sooner specialised help is put in place, the better.

CASE STUDY

Matty, age 2, has attended nursery from the age of 4 months. He appeared to pass the usual developmental milestones until his key worker noticed that he avoided playing on outdoor equipment such as tricycles, the slide or the climbing frame. When he's outside, he just runs around or sits and watches the others. He seems to have difficulties with activities that require fine motor skills such as threading, weaving and pegboards. He also finds it hard to use bats, balls and beanbags. Matty's parents and the nursery staff planned an IEP focusing on Matty's motor development, which he's been following for six months. Recently, though, he's begun to have problems at snack and meal times, finding it difficult to use his cutlery, or even to hold his beaker. At Matty's last review it was decided to refer him to the nursery's health visitor, with a view to asking for specialised help from the local physiotherapy service, or even a physical assessment to discover whether Matty has an underlying motor problem.

Continual engagement with the child and parents

The first 25 years of integration/inclusion of children with special needs has shown the enormous benefits of working closely with the parents and the child. In the early days, it's fair to say, parental involvement was often the good practice of an inspired professional rather than a requirement or legislation, but it's now regarded as the norm. The benefits shared by everyone in the team, from the child to the outside agent, include:

- a feeling of belonging
- a sense of empowerment
- possession of the facts

- openness of information

- sharing of a commitment

- reduction of anxieties

- pooling of ideas and suggestions

- confidence in knowing what to do and when

- willingness to rewrite a failing plan because of joint support.

The biggest beneficiary is the child – the reason why we're all in the game in the first place!

Focused intervention

While you have the experience and expertise gained from an overview of the wider early years picture, you may feel less confident in your knowledge of a specialised field. Even practitioners with a special needs qualification are likely to have studied one particular field of difficulty, for example learning difficulties or communication and language problems, and so would still benefit from cooperating with those outside agents who are specialists in other areas. Asking for help from an outside agent helps to sharpen up your approaches to, and perceptions of, the child's difficulties. It helps focus more specifically on methods and strategies that are likely to be effective and have a positive outcome for the child's learning and development.

CASE STUDY

Andrew, aged 4, moved house and started at the nearby nursery. Within minutes he began to behave inappropriately, being extremely aggressive towards the other children and physically assaulting them. Sometimes there was no apparent reason for his attacks. He couldn't concentrate on an activity for longer than a minute, and he skipped from one to another without completing any of them. The staff and Andrew's mother (Dad had left the family eight months previously) planned and put into place an IEP aimed at helping Andrew to develop positive behaviour, and increase his concentration. But the episodes of Andrew's aggression towards the other children increased and some of the other parents complained about his behaviour. Everybody held an early review meeting and decided to refer Andrew to the educational psychologist and the pre-school behaviour support service.

Dissemination of effective approaches and techniques

Something learned is never wasted and you'll find that, having used a specialised method with one child, you become more confident to try similar techniques with another child having difficulties. There's never a guarantee that the same technique will work for two different children, but when you work closely with the outside agent, you'll feel better about asking for, trying out and expanding on many more ways around a problem. This is much more effective than trying to go forward unsupported – if you don't know the answer, you *must* ask somebody who does, for the child's sake.

These approaches and techniques should be child centred and flexible, and Figure 7.1 highlights how this is, with the child at the nucleus of any planning. All agencies must, of course, have a system of close liaison with everybody else in the team, ensuring an interchange of ideas and information.

Figure 7.1   **Support using a child-centred approach**

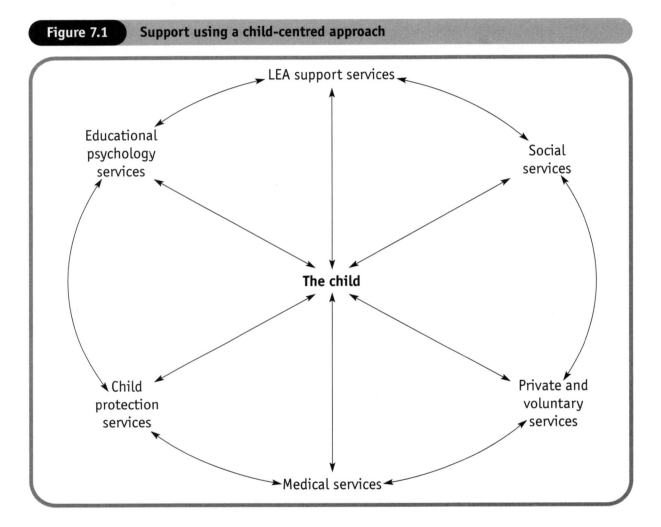

To save you a bit of time, it's useful to have a quick-reference register of which outside agents are supporting which children. It always happens that you need to phone somebody in a hurry, and you can't find the number, so you end up wading through the filing cabinet or the LEA directory, trying to locate the information you want. Having a pro forma such as Figure 7.2, an example of a completed quick-reference register, ensures that the vital statistics are instantly at hand. Like all such documentation, however, make sure it's kept somewhere out of general view.

There's a blank photocopiable version of this form on page 140.

Figure 7.2	An example of a completed quick reference register

Child's name & DOB	Outside agent(s)	Agency	Contact details
Christina Simpson 14.03.01	David Johns .... Ann Lowe	Ed. Psych .... E. Years Support	Tel. 02341 456789 Tel. 02341 567890
Manjit Kaur 31.10.00	Ann Lowe ...... Mandy Smith	E. Years Support Speech Therapist	Tel. 02341 567890 Tel. 02341 927395 ....
Jacob Nathanson 25.08.01	Dan Scott	Behaviour Support	Tel. 02341 458928 ....
	....	....	....
	....	....	....
	....	....	....

● What would be the outside agents' involvement?

I can't tell you the answer to this question! It very much depends on such things as the nature and severity of the child's difficulty, the resources available in your locality, the workload of the outside agents you call in, to name just a few variables. But by the following general exploration of the type of involvement that you're most likely to experience, you can get a flavour of what can happen after referral.

The LEA support services

The professionals from these agencies will give you advice on a number of things such as the following.

● *Teaching techniques and strategies.* You might be shown anything from a kinaesthetic approach, to circle time techniques, to a regulated step-by-step programme, to a loop induction system, to Makaton signing. There's a feast of methods, techniques, approaches and systems available to make both the child's learning and development successful and happy, and your part in this effective and enjoyable.

● *Setting management.* Sometimes we can't see the wood for the trees, and it can take a fresh pair of eyes to spot something within our setting that could be the cause of holding a child back, or preventing their full inclusion. This could be in terms of room layout, equipment and resources, timetabling, personnel, teaching approaches, or the child's learning style. You may need to do a bit of tweaking to adapt to or for any of these elements, to ensure the child receives effective support.

● *Curriculum materials.* There can be times when the child isn't motivated or stimulated by the activities on offer, and the support services can advise on materials and activities that are known to work. This doesn't mean you have to spend loads of money on re-equipping your setting. The support services may be able to lend you appropriate materials, or point you in the direction of where you can borrow them, such as a Toy Library or a centre dedicated to a specific disability.

● *Curriculum development.* You can't be prepared for all eventualities and your curriculum may not be fully geared up for inclusion in terms of specific difficulties or disabilities. Again, the appropriate support service will help you to plan the curriculum to ensure it's appropriate and effective for particular children.

● *Direct teaching or practical support for practitioners, and/or part-time specialist help.* This depends on your LEA's policy. Some support service professionals will come to your setting to work with a specific child or group of children; others will come to give you practical support, but won't necessarily work with the child themselves. How often they visit you will depend on their workload and the nature of their involvement.

● *Access to learning support assistance.* Again, this depends on your LEA's arrangements. Some authorities have Learning Support Assistants – LSAs (also known as Teaching Assistants, or TAs) who are allocated to a specific child or group of children (see below). They will either work with the child(ren) directly, or give support during larger group sessions, depending on the child's needs. Sometimes LSAs are employed by a setting and are part of the staff, to be deployed according to the setting's requirements.

The different support services can usually offer specialised help in the fields of:

● learning difficulties;

● speech and language/communication difficulties;

● sensory difficulties (visual and/or hearing impairments);

● physical difficulties;

● behaviour difficulties.

Sometimes there's a designated Early Years Learning Support Service (EYLSS), also offering specialised help, and/or a Portage scheme in place. Check what your LEA is offering – your Area SENCO will be able to tell you. The LEA should provide you with their services' contact details, but if they haven't, ask the LEA's SEN department or, again, your Area SENCO. If your setting is private or non-maintained, it's a good idea to link up with your local state-maintained early years providers to share information, facilities, services and best practice.

The child or educational psychological services

The principal practitioners in these services are educational psychologists (EPs) whose responsibilities include:

● doing more specialised assessments that focus on identifying an additional need or difficulty;

● suggesting problem-solving strategies;

● advising about behaviour-management techniques;

● evaluating the progress of individual children;

● offering information and advice about developing SEN policies;

● offering professional development in the area of SEN;

● helping to promote inclusion.

It's important to remember that some parents may become very alarmed at the mention of a psychologist, sometimes confusing the term with 'psychiatrist'. Make sure you handle the situation with sensitivity if the time comes that you need to refer a child to the EP.

Advisers or teachers of information and communications technology (ICT) for children with additional needs

Check whether your LEA has such a service – again it's a 'local thing'. There's a vast amount of hardware, software and gadgets available to provide support, learning opportunities and experiences, games and activities to assist the development of a child with additional needs. There are programs designed to support specific difficulties and the ICT support service will advise about what's appropriate for a certain child. You may not need to buy the technology since the services often lend stuff to a setting for as long as the child needs it.

Social services

There's sometimes a perception that social services become involved with a family only when it's in trouble, when there's abuse going on, or when a child has to be taken into care. But their brief is much wider, and they can offer advice and support to you and your setting, and the child's parents about other things including:

- applications for benefits or other welfare assistance;

- loan of equipment, resources or facilities;

- respite care, holiday breaks or other similar facilities;

- applications for building grants if the child's house needs adaptations;

- societies or venues offering mutual and/or self-help support;

- information on voluntary, charitable or independent bodies working in the field of specific disabilities or difficulties;

- Positive Parenting courses, offering support and counselling to parents who feel they need a bit of help themselves.

Speak to your Area Social Worker and find out what's on offer – you never know when it'll be needed.

Child protection services

It's a sad reflection on our society that we need to have these services. Your setting should have a designated child protection worker, whose job is to immediately contact the relevant authorities when abuse of any kind (physical, emotional and/or sexual, and neglect) is suspected.

Once they're involved with a family, the child protection services will liaise with you closely, to ensure the ongoing support and protection of the child. They may even become part of the team working to support the child's additional needs, so a sharing of information and skills will only be for the child's benefit.

CASE STUDY

Emily, aged 4, has an autistic spectrum disorder and goes to a mainstream nursery. She doesn't communicate with the other children and her only interaction with adults is to take their hand and put it on something she wants. Sometimes she has a severe outburst of screaming (usually during a changeover of activities) accompanied by hand flapping and head shaking from side to side.

Emily's parents say this screaming is continual at home, both day and night. Her mother is suffering from stress – with an older child, aged 6, and a baby of 5 months, life isn't easy. The team decided to ask Social services for advice and discovered that Emily's parents were entitled to a weekend's respite care for Emily once a month. This meant Emily staying with foster parents while her own family was able to enjoy a weekend together. By good fortune, Emily's key worker at the nursery was a registered foster parent with the local authority, and so Emily's respite weekends are spent with somebody she knows and trusts.

Medical services

Clearly, it depends on the nature of the child's difficulties whether and which medical services are involved. For example, a child with cerebral palsy who also has epilepsy will definitely have medical input, but a child with learning difficulties may have no medical needs at all.

You may find yourself in liaison with:

- health visitors and/or nurses
- paediatric nurses and/or paediatricians (community or hospital-based)
- child psychiatrists
- general practitioners (GPs)
- physiotherapists
- speech and language therapists
- occupational therapists
- hospital-based counsellors.

If you identify a difficulty you suspect may be medically based, you must speak to the child's parents and advise them to take the child to their GP. If a problem is diagnosed, you're likely to be initially liaising with the GP or the child's health visitor.

Learning Support Assistant (LSA) or Teaching Assistant (TA)

This practitioner may also be referred to as the child's support worker, a term used more in the early years sector. They're usually allocated to a child or, occasionally, a group of children, to provide appropriate and effective support. Their responsibilities include:

- asking the child's parents about the child's abilities, skills and needs;

- planning with the parents, the main practitioner and the SENCO, appropriate and effective IEPs, Play Plans or Differentiated Learning Plans (DLPs);

- supporting the child in a variety of situations: one-on-one, small group, whole-group sessions, with other adults, etc.;

- informing the child's parents about the child's progress;

- keeping careful records of the child's activities, sessions and learning experiences and their outcomes;

- making a contribution to review meetings;

- liaising with the main practitioner and the SENCO when preparing the educational advice required by the LEA for a Statutory Assessment referral.

You can see that these responsibilities are similar to those of a key worker within a setting, but, as a support worker, they have closer involvement with the child who has additional needs.

Private and voluntary organisations

There's a plethora of private and voluntary bodies, usually each for a designated area of disability or difficulty, which offer a valuable source of help and information. They often have information packs targeted at specific readers such as the parents, teachers or other practitioners. You'll find the staff incredibly friendly and helpful, with lots of good, practical ideas for effective support of the child, and the family.

Sometimes the information packs can be downloaded from the Internet. Do this, if you can, since it saves postage costs – many of the organisations are charitable bodies, relying on donations to keep in business and they need to keep their expenses to a minimum.

THE CHILD – THE CENTRAL CHARACTER IN THE REFERRAL

The *SEN Code of Practice* recognises that when the child is involved in the planning and implementation of programmes of work, Play Plans and/or IEPs, they're more likely to be successful and have a greater chance of making progress and learning. There are various strategies you can adopt to make sure that the child is at the centre of the whole process.

- If it's appropriate, speak to them about their difficulties in an ethos of 'We're all special in our own way; we're all good at some things; we all need help with some things'.

- Make sure they understand the targets of their IEP and Play Plan. If they can see where they're going and why, they'll be more motivated to be involved and they'll be happier.

- Explain to the child that their parents, you, everybody in the setting and they too are a team, working together to help them.

- Watch out for any stress and anxiety that assessment and review procedures may cause the child. Anxiety can develop as a result of simply not knowing or not understanding what's going on. Keep a lookout for any signs of this and talk calmly and positively to the child about it.

- Make sure they understand the role played by outside agents. It might be a bit scary for them when 'outsiders' become involved – again, try to alleviate any anxiety.

- If it's possible, ask the outside agents involved with your setting to visit occasionally, so all the children get used to them. If they can visit at drop-off or collection time so that the parents can establish a relationship with them too, then even better. This helps to reduce the perception of 'them' being 'brought in' if this becomes necessary.

- If the child is 'looked after' by the local authority and doesn't have natural parents to offer support, establish a positive and cooperative relationship with the carers. It's as crucial for the 'looked after' child to see that foster parents or house parents are involved, as it is for a child from a more traditional background. Let the child know that these adults care for them and are a valued part of the team too.

SUMMARY

The **key points** covered in this chapter were:

- The rationale behind the referral.

- The why, who and what of outside agency involvement.

- The child – the central character.

References

1 *Special Educational Needs Code of Practice* (DfES, 2001), 10:3.

Child's name & DOB	Outside agent(s)	Agency	Contact details
	. . . .	. . . .	. . . .
	. . . .	. . . .	. . . .
	. . . .	. . . .	. . . .
	. . . .	. . . .	. . . .
	. . . .	. . . .	. . . .
	. . . .	. . . .	. . . .

Glossary of some educational acronyms

BSL	British Sign Language
CoP	Code of Practice
DfEE	Department for Education and Employment (title now obsolete)
DfES	Department for Education and Skills
DLP	Differentiated Learning Plan
EP	Educational Psychologist
EYDCP	Early Years Development and Childcare Partnership (being phased out at the time of writing)
EYLSS	Early Years Learning Support Service
GP	General Practitioner
HV	Health Visitor
ICT	Information and Communication Technology
IEP	Individual Education Plan
INSET	In-service Training
IPSS	Independent Parental Support Service
LEA	Local Education Authority
LSA	Learning Support Assistant
PP	Play Plan
PPS	Parental Partnership Service
PSS	Parental Support Service
QCA	Qualifications and Curriculum Authority
SEN	Special Educational Needs
SENCO	Special Educational Needs Coordinator
SSD	Social Services Department
TA	Teaching Assistant

Further Reading

How to Survive and Succeed as a SENCO in the Primary School, Veronica Birkett (LDA, 2000).

Index for Inclusion: Developing Learning and Participation in Schools, T. Booth, M. Ainscow, K. Black-Hawkins, M. Vaughan and L. Shaw (Centre for Studies on Inclusive Education, 2000), available from the Centre for Studies on Inclusive Education, Room 2S203, 5 Block, Frenchay Campus, Coldharbour Lane, Bristol, BS16 1QU. Telephone: 01173 444 007.

Planning and Organising the SENCO Year: Time-saving Strategies for Effective Practice, Dot Constable (David Fulton Publishers, 2002).

Special Educational Needs Code of Practice (DfES, 2001).

SEN Toolkit (DfES, 2001).

All Together: How to create inclusive services for disabled children and their families. A practical handbook for early years workers, M. Dickins and J. Denziloe (National Children's Bureau, 2nd edn, 2003).

Special needs in early years settings: a guide for practitioners, Collette Drifte (David Fulton Publishers, 2001).

Early learning goals for children with special needs, Collette Drifte (David Fulton Publishers, 2002).

Handbook for Pre-school SEN Provision: the SEN Code of Practice in relation to the Early Years, Collette Drifte (David Fulton Publishers, 2003).

Encouraging Positive Behaviour in the Early Years: a practical guide, Collette Drifte (Paul Chapman Publishing, 2004).

Right from the Start: Effective planning and assessment in the early years, Vicky Hutchin (Hodder & Stoughton, 1999).

Supporting Inclusion in the Early Years, Caroline A. Jones (Open University Press, 2004).

Developing Individual Behaviour Plans in the Early Years, Hannah Mortimer (NASEN, 2000).

Taking Part, Hannah Mortimer (QEd Publications, 2000).

The Role of the Special Educational Needs Co-ordinator (SENCO) in Pre-school Settings (Pre-school Learning Alliance, 2002).

Index

assessments: 15, 70, 72, 73, 94, 97, 99, 135
   standardised assessments: 15, 94, 96
   individualised assessments: 96, 97
checklists: 98–101

Differentiated Learning Plans: 1, 27, 60, 138

expression of concern: 60, 61, 82

identifying SEN: 15, 46-52, 59
inclusion: 2, 11, 12, 13, 14, 16, 17, 28
integration: 13
Individual Education Plans (IEPs): 63–64, 65, 84
in-service training: 2, 31–34, 36–58

observations: 60, 91–94, 95
   continuous (narrative) observation: 92, 93
   focused (targeted) observation: 92, 95
outside agents: 70, 72, 81, 128, 131–138
   referral to outside agents 72, 131

parental involvement: 16, 109–127
   letters to parents: 120–125
   Parental Support Service/Parental Partnership Service: 16, 114
Play Plans: 63, 111–114

records/record keeping: 89–108
requirements for fulfilling the SENCO role: xii–xiii, 3–10
reviews: 9, 15, 66 –70, 73, 75, 80
   IEP reviews: 66–70, 75
   annual/biannual reviews: 80

SEN Code of Practice: 114–115
Statutory Assessment: 8, 37, 44, 75–81, 105
   referral for Statutory Assessment: 76